**BUSINESS OPPORTUNITY SUMMIT
NATIONAL TOUR**

Limited FREE Tickets Available. Ticket Must Be Activated. To Activate This Ticket Visit:
www.BusinessOpportunitySummit.com.au
And Insert Your

PROMO CODE: BIZBOOK

or FREECALL
1800 899 058
and quote your Promo Code to book

Ticket Value
$497.00

PAID

STUART ZADEL SEMINARS

Presents
THE ULTIMATE
BUSINESS OPPORTUNITY SUMMIT
NATIONAL TOUR

Limited FREE Tickets Available. Ticket Must Be Activated. To Activate This Ticket Visit:
www.BusinessOpportunitySummit.com.au
And Insert Your

PROMO CODE: BIZBOOK

BusinessOpportunitySummit.com.au

Please visit
BusinessOpportunitySummit.com.au
or FREECALL
1800 899 058
and quote your Promo Code to book

Ticket Value
$497.00

STUART ZADEL SEMINARS

Presents
THE ULTIMATE
BUSINESS OPPORTUNITY SUMMIT
NATIONAL TOUR

Limited FREE Tickets Available. Ticket Must Be Activated. To Activate This Ticket Visit:
www.BusinessOpportunitySummit.com.au
And Insert Your

PROMO CODE: BIZBOOK

BusinessOpportunitySummit.com.au

Please visit
BusinessOpportunitySummit.com.au
or FREECALL
1800 899 058
and quote your Promo Code to book

Ticket Value
$497.00

CLAIM YOUR FREE BONUS DVD NOW!

For a FREE copy of my detailed DVD, **"Secret Strategies You Need To Know To Make Your Fortune In Property And Keep It!"** register online at: **www.TGRProperty.com.au/FREEDVD using Promo Code: NEWPROP**

This valuable DVD captures three of Australia's top property experts live on stage revealing their closely guarded secrets.

After registering your details my free DVD will be rushed to you at no cost or obligation. This offer is valid for Australian delivery addresses only.

But you must act immediately. This FREE DVD offer is valid for a limited time only. Once the copies are gone, they're gone. So get in quick before you miss out. Register online at: **www.TGRProperty.com.au/FREEDVD** using **Promo Code: NEWPROP**

Alternatively, phone our office on **Freecall Number: 1800 899 058** during business hours OR cut out the coupon below and post to: Stuart's FREE DVD, P.O. Box 1232, SUTHERLAND NSW 1499.

☐ **Yes Stuart! Please rush me my FREE DVD** titled "Secret Strategies You Need To Know To Make Your Fortune In Property And Keep It!" [code: NEWPROP]

Please complete below in CAPITALS. Note: All fields required.

Name _____
Street Address _____
Suburb _____
State _____ Postcode _____
Email Address _____
Mobile Phone _____

Cut out your completed coupon and post to:
Stuart's FREE DVD P.O. Box 1232 SUTHERLAND NSW 1499.

HIGH PRAISE FOR STUART ZADEL'S SEMINARS

"I made in excess of $200,000 in one deal!"
"I bought a property with a valuation of $520,000 for $315,000. The process took five days and I made over $200,000 which sure beats laying bricks for a living."

Ray, Sydney

"With the skills I've learnt, I get to help people"
"I have studied and combined two of your expert's strategies, and now have the freedom to work with my laptop from home (or anywhere!). Most importantly to me, with the skills I've learnt, I get to help people who literally have no one else to turn to - plus I make incredible profits for myself. I love it!"

Wayne Firkin, Perth

"Brilliant opportunities and life changing"
"Thanks so much for a fantastic weekend, great room, buoyant energy, authentic, engaging Aussie speakers, and brilliant opportunities - life changing as usual!"

A. Burrell, Canberra

"Thank you for caring"
"Thank you seems so little, compared with what you gave me this weekend in Brisbane, but THANK YOU from the bottom of my heart. Thank you for caring enough about us and sharing such wonderful information, humour and love with us. You are an inspiration."

M. Haverty, Brisbane

"The best of the best"
"I felt the need to write to you to acknowledge how amazing the weekend event was. I have been to a couple of 'similar' events with some very successful companies (some of which I paid big money to go to) and I must say that your event was superior in many ways. Congratulations on an event that showcased amazing presenters, easy to understand information and exceptional further programmes - held together with passion, integrity and a deeper spiritual meaning."

Tracey, Greenwich

STUART ZADEL

THE <u>NEW</u> WAY TO MAKE MONEY IN BUSINESS FAST!

FREE BONUS DVD PLUS LIVE EVENT TICKETS INSIDE

© Copyright 2012 TGR Seminars Pty Ltd
This work is copyright. All rights reserved by the publisher. Apart from any use as permitted under the *Copyright Act 1968*, no part of this publication may be reproduced, stored in a retrieval system, or transmitted in any form or by any means, electronic, digital, mechanical, photocopying, recorded or otherwise, without the prior written permission of the copyright owner. Requests and inquiries concerning reproduction and rights should be addressed to: The Publisher, *The New Way to Make Money in Business Fast!*, P.O. Box 1232, Sutherland NSW 1499.

DISCLAIMER

The information, strategies, comments, concepts, techniques and suggestions within this book are of a general nature only and do not constitute professional or individual advice in any way. You must seek your own independent professional advice relating to your particular circumstances, goals and risk profile if you intend to take any action as a result of reading this publication. The publisher, authors and experts who participated in this project do not accept any responsibility for any action taken as a result of reading this publication. Every care has been taken to ensure the accuracy of the material contained in the book.

National Library of Australia Cataloguing-in-Publication entry:

The New Way to Make Money in Business Fast! / Stuart Zadel.

First published 2012
ISBN: 9780980769708 (pbk)

1. Success in business – Australia.
2. Finance, Personal – Australia.

650.1

Email: stuart@stuartzadel.com
Websites: www.stuartzadel.com
           www.BusinessOpportunitySummit.com.au/BIZBOOK

CONTENTS

Preface   1

Introduction   5

Chapter 1
Stuart Zadel
The New Business Basics   9

Chapter 2
Luke Fatooros and Alan Furlong
How To Renovate Your Business   29

Chapter 3
Dominique Grubisa
Real Estate Rescues   77

Chapter 4
Matt and Amanda Clarkson
The Magic of eBay   129

Chapter 5
Daniel Kertcher
Forex Trading   175

Chapter 6
Sean Rasmussen
Selling and Marketing Information Online   223

Chapter 7
Judeth Wilson
Being Paid to Speak   273

The Next Step…   313

DEDICATION

To all business owners past, present and future…thank you. You are the real royalty of the nation. You inspire me!

Stuart Zadel

PREFACE

A wise man once said to me: "Once you've spent your money, you can always make it back but once you've spent your time, it's gone forever."

That thought has driven me ever since - both personally and professionally.

My company was created to inspire Australians to raise their awareness, find their purpose and achieve financial freedom – fast and ethically.

You see, there are two ways to do something – the smart way or the not-so-smart way. I want to teach people the smart way because that's how to make best use of your time.

It is said: "An hour's conversation across a table with a successful person in any field is worth a whole year's reading on the subject." If you had the choice to spend an hour with someone who has achieved what you want to, or a year's study on your own, which would you choose?

If you'd choose the former – just like me – then that's why you've picked up this book.

There are common denominators of success and learning from the masters is one of them.

Scottish-born, American businessman and philanthropist, Andrew Carnegie, was once the richest man in the world, making his fortune in the steel industry.

PREFACE

He wrote an epitaph for his grave that read: "Here lies one who knew how to get around him men cleverer than himself."

In other words, he surrounded himself with people who knew more than he did; he leveraged their time and expertise. He sat on the shoulders of giants, in the process becoming one himself. That's the model my business is built on.

The New Way to Make Money in Business Fast! contains the expertise of nine business experts who have done the hard yards for you. Reading each chapter of this book is just like having a one-on-one session with its author – a successful, creative, smart business entrepreneur. How does it get any better than this?

Their proven, step-by-step strategies will work for anyone who is prepared to invest the time to learn and implement them. These members of my inner circle have made sure of it.

Which brings me to another key success indicator – the power of the mastermind team.

Wealth-generation is a team sport. As individuals, we can't possibly know all there is to know, nor do we necessarily want to. It's far easier, quicker, cheaper and more effective to build a team of experts, working in harmony towards a pre-determined goal.

Since 2006, I've been building my own team of staff and wealth-generation partners to help achieve five big goals.

We call it our 2020 Vision.

> *"Without vision, the people will perish."*
> **King Solomon**

By the year 2020 our Vision is to:

1. **Inspire 1,000 prosperity millionaires:** These millionaires come from a place of abundance; they create massive value, are charitable and leave a legacy. They create wealth for themselves and those around them. Every prosperity millionaire creates 10 jobs; every prosperity billionaire creates 10,000 jobs.
2. **Distribute one million books:** Not a week goes by that we don't receive a message from someone whose life has been transformed by one of our books. We believe strongly in the power of self-education and have already distributed more than 320,500 books in Australia and internationally.
3. **Educate 50,000 people at live seminars:** Remember, one hour learning directly from a successful person is worth a year's reading. We offer a smart learning option.
4. **Donate one million dollars to worthy causes:** The principle of tithing is not new though many consider it to be a money subtracter. I believe it is a money multiplier when carefully deployed. Think "hand up, not hand out".
5. **Plant one million trees:** I'm spiritual, not religious. But I know God encouraged us to go forth and multiply; he also instructed us to replenish the earth. I see lots of multiplying going on but not much replenishing! We think planting trees benefits everyone.

Wealth is noble, spiritual and good in the hands of noble, spiritual and good people. It cannot and will not make you something you are not; it can only take on the characteristics of the person whose hands in which it resides.

We all want to live in a wealthy nation. However, a wealthy nation is not one in which all the money is concentrated in the hands of a few. It is one in which all its citizens have the

PREFACE

opportunity to participate in abundance and drink from the well of wealth. After all, wealth is your birthright.

The information in this book can lead you to the well of wealth but only you can drink from it. I encourage you to read it from cover to cover and to learn from the masters. Allow us to join and guide you on *your* wealth-generation journey.

Now, before you even turn the page to get started, I encourage you to register for both your FREE DVD and free live event tickets, details of which are at the front of the book.

Finally, in order to transform your intention to generate wealth and develop a prosperity mindset into something tangible, download our "Prosperity Millionaire Commitment" from **www.BusinessOpportunitySummit.com.au/commitment**. Print it out and place it wherever you'll see it regularly; beside your bed, on the bathroom mirror or on the fridge door – anywhere that will remind you that you really can choose to experience financial abundance and live the life of your dreams. What else is possible?

In the meantime, I trust you will enjoy *The New Way to Make Money in Business Fast!*

Stuart Zadel

INTRODUCTION

"In times of change learners inherit the earth; while the learned find themselves beautifully equipped to deal with a world that no longer exists."

Eric Hoffer, Writer

The oldest surviving business in the world today is said to be a Finnish pulp and paper manufacturer whose first share grant dates back to 1288.

More than 720 years ago though, it was a copper mining company, diversifying into paper and pulp only in the late 19th Century. Several mergers and name changes later, it is now promoted as a "global rethinker of the paper, biomaterials, wood products and packaging industry"[1].

Not bad if we are to believe the statistics which tell us 80 per cent of small businesses fail in the first five years, and 80 per cent of those that survive five years won't make 10!

Even more shocking, only 20 per cent of businesses that still exist 10 years after start-up make decent money.

Interesting that the business above promotes itself as a "rethinker". Could that be one of the great secrets to its longevity?

Cartoonist and author Hugh MacLeod says: "All existing business models are wrong. Find a new one."

Industrialist and art collector, Jean Paul Getty, put it another way: "No one can possibly achieve any real and lasting success or 'get rich' in business by being a conformist."

---

1   www.storaenso.com

INTRODUCTION

Which brings us to *The New Way to Make Money in Business Fast!*

In this book, you'll meet nine entrepreneurs who have rethought the way business is done – and turned all previous models upside down and inside out!

Traditionally, business owners borrowed large sums of money (usually against their homes), bought a whole bunch of physical stock to sell, fitted out a premises, spent lots of money advertising - and waited for customers to arrive.

Those days are…going, going, almost gone.

Business is being battered by change thanks to the impacts of the Internet and other technology, interest rates, inflation, outsourcing, market deregulation, free trade agreements, changing demographics, fluctuating consumer confidence, workplace laws and shifting/emerging markets. Put simply, traditional business done the traditional way can't - and won't - survive.

On the other hand, the world's population continues to expand - rapidly! It doubled in just 40 years from three billion people to six billion between 1959 and 1999. It's currently just over seven billion and is estimated to reach nine billion by 2050.

That's an extra two billion people in the next four decades. All these people will need to be fed, clothed, housed, transported, educated and entertained.

So, any businesses and systems that embrace change, exploit technology and solve people's problems, smartly and efficiently, will prosper and profit from this unprecedented opportunity.

Speaking of embracing change…

Did you know it is possible to make more money in crowded markets than in businesses with few competitors?

Are you aware of how to profit professionally by helping mortgage defaulters and their creditors?

Can you imagine making a six-figure profit in just one month with no staff, stock or premises to speak of?

What about a business system that could replace your full-time wage by "working" an hour or two a day?

How does selling the world's fastest growing digital product from your keyboard or touch screen, automatically and while you sleep, sound?

Would you be surprised to know that you can use your personality and existing skills to earn $35,000 in a month while working just 10 days?

In *The New Way to Make Money in Business Fast!*, you'll discover low-risk, high-profit strategies proven by my prosperity business millionaires. They'll teach you how to replicate their systems so you, too, can explore the future of business – today.

In the first chapter, I'll reveal to you the number one concern you need to keep in mind when starting your own business. This alone will point you effortlessly towards "Due North" on the business compass, and help you navigate a safe and profitable path forward.

Next, Business Renovators Alan Furlong and Luke Fatooros will show you their Entrepreneurs Ecosystem and the seven steps to bring it to life. Together, these can potentially take your idea and turn it into $100,000 in 12 months or less, or help revive a stagnant or failing business.

In chapter three, Australia's Debt Expert and barrister, Dominique Grubisa, reveals how to profit from property in the new economy. She has developed a system to buy "distressed real estate" at substantial discounts direct from the banks.

INTRODUCTION

Then, eBay millionaires, educators and best-selling authors, Matt and Amanda Clarkson, will demonstrate to you why eBay is the fastest and easiest way anyone can create a cashflow business from home. Learn from their processes and get a piece of the $161,000,000-a-day action!

If the idea of "working" less than an hour or two per day sounds appealing, you'll love what Daniel Kertcher has to share in chapter five. A successful and innovative financial educator, he'll teach you how to trade the world's major currencies with limited investment, low risk and in an educated – not speculative – way.

In chapter six, Sean Rasmussen (recently voted one of the top 10 Internet bloggers in the world) will show you how to create products and profits "out of thin air". He lays bare the secrets, step-by-step, of selling and marketing information products on the Internet - the world's biggest ever customer database.

Finally, Judeth Wilson, corporate training and speaking guru, will show you how to leverage your personality and passion to earn up to $350,000 a year as an in-demand, highly-paid corporate trainer. Judeth will reveal which topics are hot right now and how you can get started in this rapidly growing industry.

Welcome to the savvy, smart and profitable worlds of the latest members of my personal business entrepreneurs team. Each member has generously agreed to reveal their proven systems so you can become one of our 1,000 Prosperity Millionaires.

Former US President Ronald Reagan once said: "The best minds are not in government. If they were, business would hire them away." I believe some of the best business minds are in this book – will you join them?

To your success!

Stuart Zadel

Chapter 1
THE NEW BUSINESS BASICS

"Begin with the end in mind."

STUART ZADEL

STUART ZADEL

Wealth educator Stuart Zadel is an author, speaker, publisher, entrepreneur and Director of Australia's premium wealth education company.

His purpose is to inspire people to raise their awareness, find their purpose, and achieve financial freedom.

Stuart is renowned for his authentic, humorous and sometimes controversial style that packs a powerful inspirational punch.

He has five big goals that he and his team are working towards:

1. Inspire 1,000 prosperity millionaires
2. Distribute one million books
3. Educate 50,000 people at live seminars
4. Donate one million dollars to worthy causes
5. Plant one million trees.

Combining entrepreneurship, skill, drive and his specialised knowledge of the mind-money connection, Stuart teaches more than 8,000 people each year about financial prosperity, personal leadership, sales success and peak performance.

He has authored his own series of cutting-edge wealth-creation books, and co-authored three others on sales, leadership and public speaking.

As a successful business owner for more than 20 years, Stuart also actively practices several of the strategies his wealth-generation team members teach.

He has a clear vision to encourage everyone to experience an abundant life – and uncompromising integrity.

THE NEW BUSINESS BASICS

DISCOVER TODAY'S MOST DESIRABLE BUSINESS CHARACTERISTICS AND THE TWO BIGGEST SECRETS TO BUSINESS SUCCESS

> **Alice:** *"Would you tell me, please, which way I ought to go from here?"*
> **The Cheshire Cat:** *"That depends a good deal on where you want to get to."*
> **Alice:** *"I don't much care where."*
> **The Cheshire Cat:** *"Then it doesn't much matter which way you go."*
> **Alice:** *"...So long as I get somewhere."*
> **The Cheshire Cat:** *"Oh, you're sure to do that, if only you walk long enough."*
> **Lewis Carroll,** *Alice in Wonderland*

When I was growing up, one of my favourite cartoons was called *Journey to the Centre of the Earth*. In it, a lone explorer named Arne Saknussemm made a fantastic descent to the lost kingdom of Atlantis at the Earth's core.

Centuries later his trail was accidentally discovered by some new intrepid explorers in an extinct volcano. When their exit was sabotaged by villains, they forged ahead, searching for the way out via their goal, the centre of the Earth.

Their only guide or navigation was every now and then they would find Arne's initials "A.S." inscribed on a wall with an arrow pointing the way he had gone. In much the same way, in this chapter, I wish to point the way as if with my initials "S.Z."

And just like our explorers, you won't find the sign posts standing still. You actually have to get moving in your own business.

Starting your own small business is a fantastic journey, with many twists and turns, obstacles and dangers ahead.

Allow me to share with you some lessons and suggestions from my 22 years' business and business coaching experience. In doing so, you may avoid some major pitfalls and find your way to your goal faster.

And just like Alice and our friendly Cheshire Cat in the quote above, it's better to start with the end in mind.

WHERE DO YOU WANT TO GO?
If you had all the time and money in the world, what would you do with your life? I mean, after you travel and buy things and presents and all that kind of stuff, what would you do day-to-day? Is it different to what you are doing right now? If so, I don't believe you are living your true life, and I don't believe you are truly happy.

For many, they simply don't know what they want. They say, "I know what I *don't* want!" But that's not enough. And they know it.

No meaningful good can come to you until you decide where you want to go in life, where you want to end up and what you want to experience along the way. And so most people end up just drifting along, never deciding, never winning and never really living.

And if you're not living your true life right now, what's stopping you? Seriously. Is it lack of money? Lack of time? Prior commitments or obligations? Other people? Fear? What?

THE NEW BUSINESS BASICS

The reality is it could be a few things but usually it all comes down to two: time and money.

So once you *do* have an idea of what you would like to be doing with your life, my next questions are:

- What's the likelihood of you having that kind of time and money in the next few years?
- What's your plan to get there?

I'm guessing, whatever your choice, it's going to require money – probably a whole bunch of it, to buy your time back. But just how much is enough?

HOW MUCH DO YOU WANT?

"Most people think they want a lot more money than they really need, but settle for a lot less than they could get."
Earl Nightingale

Before you decide on how much money you want, it's important to know what it's good for. One of my mentors said to me: "Money only has two purposes: to make you comfortable and to provide service."

So, how comfortable do you want to be and how much service do you want to provide?

Getting clear on each of these will also help you get clear on what sort of strategy you'll need because it will have to have the capacity to meet your targets, or lead to circumstances that do.

THE WAYS TO MAKE MONEY

For most people money's not going to just fall out of the sky in their lap or magically materialise overnight without some effort.

STUART ZADEL

Chances are you're going to have to do something to get it. So let's look at seven ways you could make money.

1. **Steal it:** Crime pays in the short term, but the risks far outweigh the rewards. Sooner or later - and usually sooner - it will catch up with you. Better to own the bank than rob it!

2. **Inherit it:** I don't know about you but I'm not the winning ticket holder of the lucky sperm bank lottery. I also don't want my relatives to die prematurely.

3. **Win it:** Odds are 1 in 1,000,000 or so. That sucks.

4. **Marry it:** OK, this could work, but it's a very specialist niche.

5. **Invest it:** Take everything you've got and put it into investments. You'll need incredible skills and a spectacular rate of return or a very, very long time.

6. **Work for it:** Possible but also usually involves a really, really long time. I'm not sure you've got that long.

7. **Start your own business:** By far your greatest return on investment – but you'll need to do some research and pick the right business model. Compared with investing your money in, say, a bank or managed fund, where you may earn between three and 30 per cent (depending on where you put it and the level of risk), an investment in your own business can make you literally hundreds of per cent or more. It's not uncommon for $20,000 or $40,000 put into a solid business idea to return millions in a few short years or less.

So if your goal is to be wealthy, odds are, you need to start your own business. Fast!

Besides, do you know any wealthy person who doesn't own their own business? I don't. Not one.

THE NEW BUSINESS BASICS

MY BUSINESS JOURNEY

My business journey started out in fitness clubs. In my late teenage years I was pursuing the dream of a sports career in football (soccer to you). With the demands of training, I thought working part-time in a gym would be a good way to pay my way and get physically stronger for my sport at the same time.

I quickly realised I loved helping people achieve results more and more, and playing football less and less. At age 19 I flew to the United States to some personal training conventions where Arnold Schwarzenegger was presenting. I can't say I met him personally or remember anything he said, but this single trip had a profound effect on me. I have worked for myself ever since.

Upon my return, I starting taking on personal training clients and had progressed into sales at the gym as well. Within two years I went full-time as a mobile trainer working one-on-one with clients at parks, gyms, and at their own homes. The money was okay but the travelling was gruelling. In my first full-time year I drove three hours a day, six days a week, 52 weeks a year. That's $3 \times 6 \times 52 / 24$ hrs = 39 days per year. Thirty-nine days I spent just sitting in my car! Can you believe that? I still can't!

That's when I decided: "I'm not going to them anymore, they're going to come to me." My brother had also become a personal trainer at that time. Fed up with the travel and in need of some starting capital, I asked him if he'd like to open a gym with me. He shrugged his shoulders in indifference. I took that as a yes, and we were away.

In 1993, we opened our own gym in the middle of the "recession we had to have". We had $20,000 in starting capital and no clients. We were good instructors, but had no experience or skill in running a gym business.

After four years we found ourselves trapped working 80 hours per week each, early mornings, late nights and no time off. After four years it was still just the two of us and we were sick, tired and burnt out.

MY SNAP POINT

One particular day I was working at the gym feeling sick as a dog. My brother was home sick in bed and couldn't come in to relieve me. When it quietened down around lunch time, I went and lay on the floor at the back of the gym under the dumbbell racks where it was cool and dark. My body was aching, my eyes were hurting, and I was praying no customers would come in! Can you imagine running a business and praying for no customers to come in and give you money? Astonishing.

But in that dark place, under the dumbbell racks of life, that's when I had my "snap" point. I resolved to no longer continue to work this way. This was not the way I was meant to live. I decided that somebody out there must know how to run a business successfully and have it serve their life, not take it. And I decided to get help.

BOOKS, MENTORS AND EDUCATION

"If you think education is expensive, you should try ignorance."
Anonymous

I quickly returned to reading business, success and marketing books. I had read lots early on, which is what got me started, but as the pressures of running a traditional business mounted, I had let that go. This time I also started to invest significant money into my business and life education with courses and workshops run by experts.

I found that as my thinking improved, so did my results. We quickly hired staff and the business began to grow. I remember resisting hiring staff for so long because of some negative comments my dad had made to me early on in the piece. Ironic, because he had only ever worked for other people in his life and had never run a business!

I then learnt to only seek the opinion of people who knew what they were talking about through demonstrated results. This is more important than it first looks and has stayed with me to this day. For example, there are only two people I talk to about money - and they have demonstrated they know more about it than me.

I also learnt that the difference between succeeding and failing was simply knowing what to do, and that meant education. I developed a personal belief that every dollar invested in well-selected education courses must return me a minimum of five. That's a 500 per cent return and why I like the expensive ones - they make me more money!

"If your business doesn't make $10,000 a month, without you, get out!"

At one particular seminar, right after my "snap" point moment, the presenter offered to sign a book for you provided you bought one. So I bought his book and joined the line, not to get my book signed, but to ask him a question about my personal situation.

I gave him a 20-second rundown and he came back to me with this: "If your business is not earning you $10,000 a month, without you, get out!" He also said: "There's simply too many other opportunities out there for you to be wasting your life away in this one."

It did the trick. I got the message and made a commitment that our gym would make me $10,000 per month, without me, within 12 months, or I'd get out. Funny thing is, in about 12 months it was making this kind of money *with* a manager running it for us! Aside from making the payments each week and some admin time, I was essentially free. P.S. Always keep complete control of the finances in your business - ALWAYS.

I have never forgotten the effect of this remarkable turnaround in my business and my life, due to the power of education. I was so grateful and excited that people actually offered their knowledge and expertise to help others.

My brother and I successfully sold that fitness club for a fantastic profit after nearly eleven-and-a-half years. We could have sold it much earlier but we wanted to beat the small business failure statistics and get to year 11!

It was this business experience that proved the greatest training ground I could ever imagine and taught me much of what I know. I have since dedicated my life to providing the best specialist wealth and business education available today to help others.

Many people now ask if I would have started that business in the same way, knowing what I know now. The answers to that question follow.

GET YOUR PRIORITIES STRAIGHT

What's your number one reason to start your own business? Many people say it's flexibility, or to be my own boss, or pride of ownership, or tax advantages. That's all well and good, but how much flexibility, pride, and tax breaks will you have if you do *not* make a profit?

Let's all agree that making a healthy profit is paramount, but there's something even more important, and it's best to get this right before you start. I know a lot of business owners doing

THE NEW BUSINESS BASICS

really well financially, but sacrificing their health, relationships and other areas of their life to get it. And it's not their fault. The traditional business model will suck the very life out of you if you let it.

What traditional business owners don't have is time. Time to do the things they really want to do, to travel, spend time with family, hobbies, these sorts of things. I think "time freedom" has become the new wealth.

Remember, no one on their death bed said they wished they'd spent more time at the office!

Business should increase your life, not diminish it. Therefore your number one priority in starting a business should always be LIFESTYLE. This is your guiding compass, your Due North in all your decisions, most importantly in selecting the sort of business you want to start.

Here's my hierarchy of priorities when starting a business:

1. Lifestyle
2. Profits
3. Tax advantages.

Notice where profits sit in my hierarchy? Life is primary, money is secondary. And *making* money is more important than tax advantages.

I recall a carefree guy from my early gym days who would stroll in and casually exercise around midday. Intrigued, I made a point of getting to know him. Over time he shared with me that all he did was import a container of toys every couple of months and on-sell it to a big chain supplier for about a $70,000 profit per container. Now there's a guy who had his priorities in the right order!

AND THEY'RE RACING...
So once you're clear on what you want and why you're doing it, it's time to look at what sort of business to start. BEWARE: Not all businesses are created equal. Doing traditional business the traditional way is like riding a donkey in the Melbourne Cup. I don't care how good a jockey you are, you're never going to win! In the new economy, you need a "racehorse" business to give yourself an advantage over all the donkeys.

So what makes a "racehorse" business? Well, for starters, how about no or few staff, no premises, low or even no start-up capital, portability, can operate anywhere, anytime, large and growing worldwide markets, no face to face selling, potentially limitless profits...

I'm sure you're thinking, "Do such businesses even exist?" Yes! And I want to prove it to you. But before I do, let's look a little more closely at some of the major desirable characteristics I'd look for when establishing a new business today.

LOW START-UP COSTS: Low start-up costs equal lower risks. One of the smartest ways to lower your risk is to start a business that doesn't require significant start-up capital. This is both profitable and motivating as you'll also see a faster return on your capital.

So when people ask me if I'd start my gym today, the same way my brother and I did in 1993, the answer is a resounding no. The same business today could easily cost between $300,000 and $800,000 to establish (in fact, a new fitness club in my local area reportedly cost $2 million recently just to open the doors) and that's simply not a risk I'd be willing to take. I love gyms and "gym people" but from a strictly financial point of view, the start-up costs including equipment, rent, bonds, insurance and labour are not things I'd like to be responsible for.

THE NEW BUSINESS BASICS

LOW RUNNING COSTS: As well as low start-up costs, I like businesses with low running costs. It's not much good having a business that turns over great money but has really high overheads. That's called being a rat on a wheel!

The other day I complemented another business owner on the luxury European car he drives. He agreed it was beautiful but bemoaned: "It's nice but the running costs are killing me. The service costs and high octane fuel are ridiculous." That's just like running a business high in overheads. It might look sexy and nice on the outside, but it'll eat you up on the inside.

Remember, the game is never how much you make, but how much you keep.

LITTLE OR NO STAFF: Business is simple, people are complex - or at least unpredictable. The more staff you have the more mouths you have to feed, and the more variables that can go wrong. In all my years of business coaching, staff issues are easily the most common complaints I hear. Sometimes staff can even be downright dangerous if they try to exploit workplace law. Best to choose a business that requires few staff. Better still, avoid them altogether; outsource everything you can.

HIGH PROFIT MARGIN PRODUCTS AND SERVICES: There needs to be a good margin or mark-up to give your business the best chance of success. Let's compare cars and information products. Cars cost a lot of money but there's very little margin in them, particularly for the salesperson. Just look at all the car dealerships closing down on any main road. With skinny margins, just a small drop in the economy (or rise in the Australian dollar) can wipe you out of business. Now compare that to selling information products like software that often have lower price points but mark-ups of 1,000 per cent or more. This gives you more breathing space to add more value, provide better service and withstand a few mistakes or market movements.

FLEXIBLE/LEVERAGED TIME: Our gym was open 6am-9pm weekdays and 8am-5pm on weekends. Long hours are tough, especially when you have no staff or they're expensive when you do. Look for a business where the times are flexible or can be highly leveraged and started in your spare-time.

HIGHLY AUTOMATED/SYSTEMISED: Operating a business should be boring; get your kicks elsewhere. Business should be a repeatable process that produces a predicable financial result. And that means systems. Businesses that can be highly systemised and automated do three things:

1. Eliminate mistakes and provide consistency
2. Buy back your time
3. Become very desirable assets for investors to buy.

Even if you never wish to sell, you can train someone or outsource the steps if it is highly systemised.

PORTABLE: When talking lifestyle, a lot of people like the idea of travel. Therefore, it's good to start a business that allows you to travel without being tied to a particular geographical location. This way, you can travel and still run it while on the road or do business wherever you go. Of course, if you don't like the economic climate or government taxes, you can always just move somewhere warmer!

GROWING WORLD MARKET/RISING TIDE:

In Shakespeare's *Julius Ceasar*, Act IV, Scene III, it reads;

> *"There is a tide in the affairs of men,*
> *Which, taken at the flood, leads on to fortune;*
> *Omitted, all the voyage of their life*
> *Is bound in shallows and in miseries.*
> *On such a full sea are we now afloat;*

THE NEW BUSINESS BASICS

*And we must take the current when it serves,
Or lose our ventures."*

All boats rise and fall with the tide - and businesses do too! Not all parts of an economy grow at the same speed. Some are expanding while others are contracting. You want to float your boat (business) in a rising tide, or even better, a flood. A good example of this at the time of writing is the mining industry in Australia. Unprecedented high commodity prices coupled with unprecedented world demand have created a once-in-a-lifetime opportunity.

In a rising tide you're not trying to create the demand because it already exists in a big way. All you need to do is supply it. Therefore, logic says anything to do with the support and supply of mining services and products is likely to do really well. It could be a good idea to take the business systems presented in this book and apply them to the mining industry. Aside from mining, there are dozens of rising tides right now. The skill is to be able to spot them or anticipate them. Do you know what they are?

The above list is by no means comprehensive but it's an excellent start in the new business basics. Remember, donkeys are slow and made to carry heavy things; racehorses are fast, light, nimble and not weighed down. With a racehorse business, even a bad jockey can win. The vehicle is everything - start a thoroughbred business.

HOUSTON WE HAVE LIFT-OFF!

Did you know that space shuttle spends 80 per cent of its fuel getting into space? Once there, apparently it can be pulled by a thread. Even your racehorse business is going to require some fuel to get it off the ground, but it will be worth the effort. In fact, it could make you a millionaire…and it will if you commit.

STUART ZADEL

So before we go any further, it's time for you to make a commitment. You see, if all you do is read this book and then take no action, what's the point, right? So let's now take a moment to make it tangible. For me, inspiring 1,000 new Prosperity Millionaires, dedicated to contributing a portion of their wealth and energies to worthwhile projects, as part of our 2020 Vision, is a goal worth striving for. By doing so, we will achieve our purpose of raising the conscious and financial awareness of the planet. I'm inviting you to join us. I'm asking you to become one of our next Prosperity Millionaires. What'll it be? Yes or No?

Now make that commitment by signing here:

Stuart Zadel's Prosperity Millionaire Commitment

I _____ (name) hereby make an irrevocable commitment to becoming a Stuart Zadel Prosperity Millionaire, so that I can attain total financial freedom, serve, inspire and share my success with others and live a full life.

_____
Signed

_____ / _____ / 20 _____
Date

Next I want you to go to www.BusinessOpportunitySummit.com.au/commitment and download your free Stuart Zadel Prosperity Millionaire Certificate. Print out several copies, fill them in and place them where you'll see them around your home or workplace many times a day.

As US success author, Napoleon Hill wrote, "Somewhere in your make up (perhaps in the cells of your brain) there lies sleeping, the seed of achievement, which if aroused and put into action, would carry you to heights, such as you may never have hoped to attain."

THE NEW BUSINESS BASICS

That seed has now been planted. It has begun…

TWO SECRET KEYS FOR BOTH DONKEYS AND RACEHORSES

Some of you reading this book will already be in business, looking to improve it. So, for the benefit of both existing and future business owners here are two secret keys to wealth through business.

SECRET ONE:
THE MONEY IS IN THE…

Pssst, you deserve to know a secret - a secret that 99 per cent of business owners don't know. And before I give it to you, you should also know this secret is so powerful that at first it could really upset you, even make you mad, or really confused, or, as is more often the case, you could completely miss it all together.

Are you ready? You're sure? OK, here it is…

There is no money in *doing* what you do, that is, supplying the goods or services that you offer. All the money is in the marketing, not the *doing*. As a result, you are not in the business you think you're in. Irrespective of what product or service you provide, you are really in the business of selling and marketing. Did you get that?

Let me clarify. So an electrician is not in the electrical business. S/he is actually in the business of marketing electrical services. This may seem like a play on words, or even a subtle shift, but it's not. It's the entire ball game! There is little money in being an electrician (although they earn a decent hourly rate) when compared to being the business owner who knows how to market electrical services. The difference is significant and the financial compensation between the two is huge! Get this and you'll win. Miss it and you're doomed to be a jockey on a donkey.

SECRET TWO:
YOU'LL NEVER MAKE AS MUCH MONEY RUNNING YOUR BUSINESS AS YOU WILL SELLING IT!

I started this chapter with my quote, "Begin with the end in mind." For many, selling their business is the ultimate and this chapter simply would not be complete without this secret. It's the Grand Daddy of them all. If you want to generate some serious cash, then why not sell the very thing that generates it for you?

Selling your business can be a very profitable and rewarding thing to do. It could easily sell for between two and three times net profit and sometimes five times or more. There are a number of typical formulas used to value and price a business, but regardless of the method the truth remains: you will never make as much money running your business as you will selling it.

If you build a business to the point where you can list (sell) it on the stock market (a difficult but popular exit strategy) it can sell for 10 or 20 times earnings and in some cases 100 times. This is called the Price to Earnings Ratio, or P/E Ratio, which divides the price of a stock by its earnings per share and reveals the value of a company relative to other companies in that particular sector.

Stock market aside, wasn't the whole point of going into business to make more money and enjoy a better lifestyle? This strategy could certainly put some cash in your pocket and buy you some time to consider your next move.

Even if you don't intend to actually sell your business, you should run it as though you do. You should have the end in mind and be preparing to sell your business for a pre-determined price.

THE NEW BUSINESS BASICS

You then set about making that happen, and if you choose not to sell it, you will have built a far more valuable asset. It's wise to go through the whole process of selling your business with a reputable, professional business broker. They will tell you everything you need to do to sell it, including who your most likely buyer might be, how much your business is worth and how your industry values businesses. Armed with this information you can then take the steps necessary to increase the value of you business in a very short period of time.

BEWARE THE MONEY TRAP

"Happier is the man who lives in a tent with the person he loves, than the man who lives in a mansion all by himself."
Anonymous

Money for money's sake is a fool's game. Donating your life for digits in a bank account is an empty and lifeless pursuit. A person that is financially rich, but bankrupt in any or every other area of their life, to me, is not a success.

Sadly, most people need a few million dollars to realise you don't need that much at all to be happy. But that's something you're going to have to experience for yourself. It's a well documented fact in "happiness studies" that the worlds' happiest people are often the poorest financially. I've certainly experienced this is Thailand and have heard similar reports from Cuba.

Still, the fact remains, we live in a monetary society and if you are going to have worries, they may as well be over too much money than too little! Just keep in mind the words of Henry Ford: "A business that makes nothing but money is a poor kind of business."

CONCLUSION

When I started my business I didn't give much thought to the model. Just like carrying a flash torch in a blizzard, I could only see a few feet in front of me. And whilst it's true I wouldn't open a gym today as it doesn't meet my "new business basics", I can't tell you the satisfaction I get knowing that it's still going strong to this day, employing people and giving more life and vitality to its members. It's won awards and my time there laid the foundations for my greater success today and I am proud to say my brother and I generated that. Every physical object on planet Earth either generates something, reflects something or absorbs something. When you're gone, what will you have generated?

In the next six chapters you'll discover six of the best on-trend racehorse business opportunities available right now to make you more money in less time. Will you climb on board?

FREE BONUS GIFT

Stuart Zadel has generously offered a FREE BONUS GIFT valued at $1,491

Three (3) FREE tickets (worth $497 each) to **The Ultimate Business Opportunity Summit National Tour.**

Visit the website below to receive this free gift
www.BusinessOpportunitySummit.com.au/BIZBOOK

Chapter 2
HOW TO RENOVATE YOUR BUSINESS

"With a little help, your little acorns really can grow into mighty oaks."

LUKE FATOOROS AND ALAN FURLONG

LUKE FATOOROS AND ALAN FURLONG

The Business Renovators was founded by Luke Fatooros, serial entrepreneur, and Alan Furlong, one of Australia's leading online and offline marketing experts. Together they have created cutting edge business success mentoring models – "The Seven Steps To Business Success" and "The Facebook for Business Boot Camps" - to help businesses adapt and thrive in today's ever changing environment.

The Business Renovators was handpicked to appear live on stage in Australia with Sir Richard Branson, where they presented their ground-breaking, seven-step Entrepreneurs' Ecosystem that explains, in detail, how to take an idea from zero to $100,000 in 12 months or less.

About Luke: Luke co-founded his first business at the age of 23. Starting out in his father's shed, together with his partner, he turned $800 into a $12 million company with 65 staff within five years. He was awarded the Ernst & Young Entrepreneur's Award at 25 and the Microsoft Top 5 Companies Award at 26. Then Luke created a company valued at $3.5 million dollars, from a home office, working just two days a week, in less than three years. Luke has over 15 years' hands-on experience building businesses in South Africa, Australia, New Zealand, the USA and Canada.

About Alan: Alan has more than 23 years' sales and marketing experience. In the last four, he has focused solely on online marketing, helping countless business owners and budding entrepreneurs make more money online. He achieved financial independence through his online activities in eight months from scratch, created a (just under) six-figure launch for a client in less than two weeks, created a membership site that was generating five figures a month from day one, and has helped scores of business owners make their first online sales via their websites. He also has an MBA and has worked at a senior executive position in banking and sales.

HOW TO RENOVATE YOUR BUSINESS

SEVEN SIMPLE STEPS TO TAKE YOUR IDEA AND TURN IT INTO $100,000 IN 12 MONTHS OR LESS

> *"I went to the woods because I wished to live deliberately, to front only the essential facts of life, and see if I could learn what it had to teach, and not, when I came to die, discover that I had not lived."*
> **Henry David Thoreau, 1854**

Are you stuck? Are you in a job you hate and much to your frustration, you were sure this one was going to be different to the previous three jobs you've had? Do you want out of the terrible "work hard, live for your weekend" trap but have no idea where to start?

Are you in a job you like or enjoy but realise it is not giving you the income you deserve and, as a consequence, limiting your choices on important things like the kind of house your would like to own, the car you'd love to buy, the parent you want to be and the holidays you'd love to take?

Maybe you have a brilliant business idea but don't know how to get it off the ground? Or are you a business owner busting your butt 14 hours a day, trapped in a business that is making okay money but you never have the time or energy to enjoy it?

If you fall into any of the above brackets then this powerful, revolutionary chapter is for you.

If you want to know exactly how to find a profitable idea, or take a profitable idea from zero and turn it into $100,000 in 12 months or less, you're in the right place.

Are you intrigued? Then let's begin.

For a business to be successful, sustainable and make money long term, three critical components are required. Together these form what we call the Entrepreneurs' Ecosystem. This system is unlike anything you may have read before and it is at the heart of why we are able to achieve such astonishing success for our clients in such a short space of time.

The three components are:

1. Your "Why"
2. Your "Knowledge Centre"
3. Your "Priorities Rank".

Like any ecosystem, this one has to have all three components in balance and harmony to survive and thrive; and when you have them all working together, your Entrepreneurs' Ecosystem automatically breeds success. If any of these components is missing your ecosystem breaks down and you never succeed and enjoy long-term wealth.

YOUR "WHY"

> *"It takes a touch of genius - and a lot of courage - to move in the opposite direction."*
> **Albert Einstein**

Who believes success begins in your mind? Well actually for your Entrepreneurs' Ecosystem to work your SUCCESS NEEDS TO BEGIN IN YOUR HEART!

HOW TO RENOVATE YOUR BUSINESS

To build a successful, sustainable business that will create real long-term wealth, you need to understand WHY you are in business, not simply WHAT you do or sell.

Your mind provides the WHAT but your HEART provides the WHY.

You see, your mind looks for logic (THE WHAT) while your heart seeks purpose (THE WHY). If you drive your business solely using your mind, here's what happens: mind-based processing leads to self-imposed anchors that restrict growth. Mind-based processing limits COURAGE and MOMENTUM. That's why so many people never ever get going, that's why they can't commit to taking action; they never get traction or never get to that next level!

When you drive your business from your heart you kick-start your Entrepreneurs' Ecosystem – you begin to bring it to life and your success cycle begins with a powerful foundation. Your heart will always seek purpose. If you seek purpose for what you do, rather than rely solely on processing logic, your passion will naturally attach itself to your purpose.

Passion is your greatest driving force! Passion is a divine thrust. If you have not yet discovered how to tap into your passion, your journey has not yet begun. So passion gives you MOMENTUM to keep going and not give up when the road gets rocky.

Purpose gives you the COURAGE to do what you need to do to be successful.

When you combine a clear purpose with your passion, you create your powerful WHY.

So our first question is: what is your WHY?

Here are some typical answers:

- "I want more freedom."
- "I want more time with my family."
- "I don't want to work so hard anymore; I just want to be lazy once in a while."
- "I don't want to worry about the bills or about the mortgage payments."
- "I want to be proud of who I am; I don't want to be average anymore."
- "I want to be all that I can be."

When Luke and I set up the Business Renovators we had two primary goals. The first was to make a contribution to our clients' lives so they achieved their financial goals and personal dreams. The second, as a consequence, was to make cash to build our business, allow us to touch more lives and therefore make a bigger contribution to many more business owners and budding entrepreneurs.

My biggest personal "why" is as follows. When I first started out as an entrepreneur, I didn't want to have to worry about money like my parents had to do in the past. I also didn't even want to have someone deciding my future for me. I swore I would never allow a boss to dictate how and when I lived my life. Finally, I wanted to be proud of the person I am, rather than feeling I have settled for less than I could be in this world.

The reason this "why" is so important to me is because I saw my father's factory shut down by bailiffs two weeks before he was due to retire, after over 50 years' hard work to provide for his family. That broke my heart and I swore I would never allow anyone to do that to me or, if possible, to anyone in my family.

HOW TO RENOVATE YOUR BUSINESS

Here's Luke's "why". Luke started out as a junior engineer after graduating from university. But after just six months of being an employee, he realised he could never achieve his dreams. He realised that by being an employee, he was just another cog in the engine, helping to build someone else's life and dreams.

Luke wanted to build his own dream - a dream that would enable his family to enjoy time together, never have to worry about money, all while doing what he truly enjoyed doing.

Luke's greatest "why" is that he never wanted to sit down with his children and grandchildren one day and say, "I should have or I could have but I chose not to." He wanted his children to be proud of their dad and to say he had the courage to go out, grab his own dreams and never surrender.

Understanding our "whys" has ensured nothing has stopped either of us achieving what we wanted to.

Luke lost his first $12 million business and had to start again from scratch. He rebuilt a business valued at $3.5 million in less than three years. The reason he was able to do this was because he understood his "why". He focused on his "why", not on the money.

Understand this very profound principle and we believe your money will automatically follow. Remember your money will follow your "why", not the other way around.

YOUR "KNOWLEDGE CENTRE"
So many businesses fail, not because the idea is flawed but because the knowledge to create wealth from it does not exist. You need the right kind of knowledge to ensure your ability matches your ambition to create long-term sustainable wealth.

Even more importantly, you need to know what to do with your knowledge to make big money. Believe it or not, many business people do not know how to make big money from their businesses. They work so hard yet they leave so much money on the table for competitors! This is where your KNOWLEDGE CENTRE comes in.

How many people do you know who attend seminar after seminar, read hundreds of books and are walking encyclopedias of knowledge but never, ever make big money in the real world?

The reason this is the case is because knowledge by itself is useless. You need to know how to turn your knowledge into gold! You need to know how to make your knowledge work for you, making you money consistently and passively! This should be the goal of your knowledge.

The KNOWLEDGE CENTRE provides a VISUAL ROADMAP or BLUEPRINT of what information and knowledge you need at what point along your journey to make big money in business.

Remember success is a journey. Success is not something that lands on your doorstep if you meditate hard enough. Success awaits every single one of us, but it's up to us to embark on our journey to reach it. For some it could be just days or hours away, others maybe a bit longer but it is definitely there waiting for you to collect it. Are you in? Will you join us on this incredible journey?

Now to ensure we don't get lost on this journey we need an up to date map, our very own GPS, our KNOWLEDGE CENTRE that:

- ensures you have the correct knowledge in order for you to make big money and to ensure your level of knowledge matches your ambition through each stage of your business growth; and

- provides a step-by-step road map or blueprint of what piece of knowledge you should be using at each step of the development of your business so you see results and start reaping the rewards quicker.

The final part of your Entrepreneurs' Ecosystem that we believe ensures you'll attract more success, faster and with more ease is...

YOUR "PRIORITIES RANK"
We would all agree that none of us has more than 24 hours in a day each. No one has more time in the day than anyone else – correct? We are all busy, we all have limited resources and all of us have a very short time on this earth to make our dreams come true.

So it makes perfect sense then, that the quicker we reach our dreams and our lifestyles of choice, the more time we will have to enjoy them.

So how come some people are able to achieve so much in such a short space of time? How come they can make so much money, year after year, with such little resource, time and time again, while others continuously struggle, year after year, and never seem to get off the ground or reach that next level?

Some people are able to build multi-million dollar businesses from very little cash. Luke built his first business from just $800 and turned it into a multi-million dollar business in just five years. Others get wiped out and owe hundreds of thousands of dollars yet they are still able to bounce back from this massive debt and build massive businesses. Why?

The answer is your PRIORITIES RANK.

When you look at the individuals closely you realise it's not about time and money, it's what you DO with your time and your money that makes all the difference. These different actions you take are all part of your PRIORITIES RANK.

Do the right things with your time, spend your money on the right things, tap into the right resources and hang around with the right people who will help you get rich - these are high priorities.

These should fill up your PRIORITIES RANK and should replace your time bandits that drain you, make you unprofitable and create negative consequences that prevent you from reaching your dreams!

When your PRIORITIES RANK is correctly designed and executed, we believe your business will suddenly take off at a rate you could never imagine and you start to see MORE CASH, BIGGER RESULTS, FASTER!

The first and most important step in having a powerful priorities rank is creating your first monthly money goal.

To ensure this is realistic and achievable (particularly for new entrepreneurs) we suggest you add up your top four household bills and set that dollar amount as your first financial target. This will ensure that every action you take every day, every week and every month is geared towards achieving this first financial target.

Once you achieve that target, double that amount and set that as your next target and so on. This is how you achieve success,

HOW TO RENOVATE YOUR BUSINESS

one step at a time. If you tell us you want to make $50,000 a month, we'll ask you first to show us how you'll make $500.

So there you have the ENTREPRENEURS' ECOSYSTEM and when you have all three of these components working harmoniously, we believe your business begins to grow at an accelerated rate. Financial targets are smashed, your time is freed up, your quality of life improves, you get more balance and you gather unstoppable momentum.

The big question is, how do I bring my ecosystem to life? What are the first steps on the path? What is the map, the blueprint? What we'll share with you now are the first core elements of that path. These seven steps are at the heart of our success in business and are critical for you to master if you wish to turn your idea into a $100,000 business.

So let's begin with Step One.

STEP ONE:
DISCOVER YOUR NATURAL TALENTS/GIFTS/ABILITIES/PASSION

If you want to make money quickly and easily, always play to your strengths.

A fish that tries to climb a tree will inevitably fail! Similarly a bird that tries to become a great swimmer will never achieve success!

Every one of us has been given unique talents, strengths, gifts and abilities. Many of us have not yet discovered these or we have never allowed the magnificent giant within us to emerge!

So let's take a look at how we begin to awaken our precious gifts.

The best way to extract your hidden gold is to begin by making a list as follows:

MY SKILLS

To discover your skills, ask yourself the following questions:

- What have been my work responsibilities?
- What did I excel at, at work, school and/or sport?
- What have I studied?

MY TALENTS

To discover your talents, ask yourself the following questions:

- What comes easily to me?
- For what have I won awards and contests, and received praise?
- What gifts do I have that make others say, "I wish I could do that as well as you"?

MY PASSION

To discover your passion, ask yourself the following questions:

- What do I love to do?
- What do I do that makes time fly because I am having so much fun?

From these lists you have created, you can now start to formulate ideas for your business. Make a final list now of Potential

HOW TO RENOVATE YOUR BUSINESS

Business Ideas. List at least five (in order of preference where one equals your top choice).

Skills/Talents/Abilities	Potential Business Ideas
1. Flower arrangements	Online gift store
2. Landscaping	Upmarket garden service
3. Electronic repairs	Appliance repair centre
4. Baking	Cooking classes/book/website
5. Customer service	Virtual assistant
6. Data entry	Virtual assistant
7. Bookkeeping	Bookkeeping Service

ACTION STEPS
Create a list of your skills, talents and abilities and write down at least five business ideas from that list.

....

....

....

....

....

This next piece is vitally important - it's a golden secret to making money from your natural abilities or your passion. The most critical question you must now answer is, "Is my business idea lucrative?" because not every idea will make you money.

How do you know if it will be lucrative? Let's explore this a little deeper right now.

STEP TWO:
DISCOVER POTENTIAL CA$H IDEAS THAT MATCH YOUR STRENGTHS IN A "RED-HOT" NICHE

Here is how you are guaranteed to fail in creating your $100,000 business. It sounds something like this:

> "Hi Alan and Luke, I have an amazing idea for a business and I want to run it past you guys. I talked to my friends and family about it and they think it's fantastic. I'm so excited about this product and idea and I just know it's going to work."

Two months later, we don't hear from that person any more, their idea has crashed, their enthusiasm has disappeared and they don't understand where they went wrong.

Not every idea is lucrative. First you have to discover if your idea is actually going to make you money. Merely taking an idea and following sound business principles will not guarantee success. Why?

Because the profitability of your idea is directly proportional to your customers' willingness to actually pay for it. It does not matter how fantastic your business plan is. What matters is how willing your customers are to hand over their cash to pay for your product or service.

So here are two golden rules to ensure your idea makes you cash, quick!

1) Never create an idea and then try to find a market to sell it to.

HOW TO RENOVATE YOUR BUSINESS

2) Rather, find where customers are ALREADY spending cash easily. We refer to this as "discovering the sweet spot" within a red-hot niche!

How do you discover a red-hot niche? This process is very simple.

First take your list you created in Step One and alongside each of your ideas, list the top three competitors in that industry. For example:

Skills/Talents/ Abilities	Potential Business Ideas	Top Three Competitors
1. Flower arrangements	Online gift store	1. Sue's Gift Baskets 2. Interflora 3. Flowers&Gifts.com
2. Landscaping	Upmarket garden service	1. Tims Garden Services 2. Grande Landscaping 3. Butler Garden Designs

Why are we doing this?

You want to find business ideas where there is lots of competition! Yes, you did read correctly - where there is lots of competition! Businesses go where the cash lies. You want to find where customers are already spending money. This is a red-hot niche and you want to find the top three competitors in that niche because if they are at the top, they are making money and you want to be where the money is!

Now I can hear all of you shouting, "But surely you want no competition or very little competition?" No, you don't. The chance of you spotting a lucrative "hole" in the market where there is no competition is almost zero. The risk factors are just too high. If there is a "hole" in the market, there are very good reasons why it is still a "hole". It's because the "hole" has been explored and the customers are not prepared to pay for the service or product. So while it may appear to be a great opportunity, chances are many businesses have tried to "fill the hole" before you and failed.

Remember there are over seven billion people in the world now. The chances of you coming up with a unique business idea that no one else has thought of are slim to negligible. The reality is that if there aren't any competitors, it's because there is no money to be made with that idea.

ACTION STEPS

Identify your top three competitors for at least three business ideas.

....

....

....

What are their strengths?

....

....

....

What are their weaknesses?

....

....

....

> How do they market themselves to their customers?
>
> ....
>
> ....
>
> ....

A far easier and smarter way to accelerate your idea into a positive cash business is to find an established market, where there is lots of competition and the cash is already flowing. This is how you discover a potential red-hot niche to match your ideas.

Again, I can hear you all shouting at me, "But if there is lots of competition, how do I compete?"

Easily - which takes us to Step Three.

STEP THREE:
BECOME THE "GO-TO" TRUSTED EXPERT

> *"Most of the successful people I've known are the ones who do more listening than talking."*
> **Bernard M. Baruch, American economist**

Once you've discovered your red-hot niche and have identified the top competitors in that niche, you need to do two things to ensure you create a "go-to" market message that ensures you STAND OUT from the crowd.

Firstly, you need to deeply understand the customers who shop with your top competitors and who will be potentially shopping with you. This process helps you get crystal clear on your target market that is ready and willing to pay you cash.

Secondly, you need to understand your customers pain, anger and frustrations and become the PAINKILLER or SOLUTION PROVIDER for them.

Let's take a look at the first point - identifying your target market. Ask yourself who is going to listen to your message and, more importantly, come banging on your door with cash in their hands once they've heard it?

When Apple created the iPod they initially attracted the "techies" of the world, not the average person in the street (the techies were the only ones who understood the gadget when it was first released). The average person in the street took a couple of years or so to catch on to the iPod phenomena and the rest, as they say, is history.

So who are your "techies"; who is your target market and have you listened closely to understand what they really want?

Often when Luke and I talk to entrepreneurs, particularly experienced entrepreneurs, they talk about their target market as "everyone" and then wonder why their marketing is so expensive, their net new customers attracted from that marketing is low and the profitability of their business is terrible.

Let me give you a specific example. When Katie Prendegast came to see us, she had left employed life, set up her own business and had made a good start but wanted to really lift her sales as they just weren't happening for her.

Katie, as a speech pathologist, was skilled in dealing with her particular customers and also had excellent interpersonal skills but struggled in her new venture because of her lack of business and marketing skills.

HOW TO RENOVATE YOUR BUSINESS

As Katie's grandmother became older and frailer, she began having difficulty swallowing. This was a particularly traumatic experience for both her grandmother and her family. This "problem" (pain) led Katie to look for a solution such as thickened drinks and shakes that were easy to swallow but provided the right amount of nutrition for her grandmother. It was extremely challenging to find the right information and the right advice and that's when Katie realised she had stumbled on a red-hot niche market with a problem that she could solve.

Katie set up a website for family members, non-medical professionals and medical professionals who dealt with those individuals who struggled to swallow. Is this a red-hot niche market? Yes, absolutely.

Do they have a clear problem they need solving? Yes again. They need access to products but also access to advice about which product would be best for their family member or patient.

Katie's solution: she built a one-stop shop website that provides both products and advice to her customers. With our help, in her first 12 months she grew that small website into a business averaging $9,000 per month in sales and that equates to over $108,000 a year. And the fantastic news is, she's about to enter her next stage of growth and profitability as her business continues to grow and expand each and every week.

This all came from identifying a red-hot niche market, working out the problem of that market, then providing a solution for the customer whilst positioning herself as the go-to expert.

Remember the iPod was an evolution of the personal music player; Apple did not set out to create a whole new market from scratch. And if you think the iPad was a revolutionary product, remember again that tablets had been around for some time before Apple created it. What Apple did was make it very easy to use, incredibly functional and very "cool". So once again Apple saw a target market, identified weaknesses in their competition, solved that problem for the consumer, and become the go-to company for that product.

At this point your grey matter should be starting to work really hard, which is great and, more importantly, you should be thinking of the customer first and not your idea first.

ACTION STEPS

Looking at Katie's example, can you identify one or two potential target markets for your product or service?

....

Are those target markets willing to pay you cash?

....

Are there competitors in that marketplace and are they making a lot of profit?

....

....

Within that target market are there problems that you have identified that you can solve better, faster, cheaper, more effectively than your competition and position yourself as the go-to expert?

....

HOW TO RENOVATE YOUR BUSINESS

Now let's explore the second point a little closer - you need to understand your customers pain, anger and frustrations and become the PAINKILLER or SOLUTION PROVIDER for them.

Find a problem in your target market that you can solve; never create a product that you have to push out into the market.

So let me ask you a question. If you had a heart problem would you head off to see a General Practitioner or would you book an appointment to see a Cardiologist, an expert who has spent years learning everything there is to know about hearts?

Simple question and clearly we would all head off to see the heart specialist.

Why?

Well, the reason I would see a Cardiologist is because I want to know that I am talking to an expert, a person who has spent years and years building his skills and expertise and can solve my problem (pain) – a person I can trust when it comes to making big decisions around my health and wellbeing.

So here is my next question. Why wouldn't you apply this same philosophy to your business?

Let me explain what I mean by giving you a specific example.

Recently I was in Perth, Western Australia, to speak to a group of entrepreneurs about how to quickly and effectively build their businesses using low-cost, low-risk strategies. Whilst walking around the city I came across a bicycle shop, or what was left of it (it had recently closed down). There were a few posters left in the abandoned shopfront and it was certainly in a prime retail space in the centre of town, so how come it was no longer in business?

I ask that question because according to the statistics in Australia, bicycles have out-sold cars every year since 2009. So this is clearly a growing market and therefore the answer to the question must lie elsewhere - it was clearly not a demand issue.

Fast-forward two weeks and I was wandering around Sydney with Luke and we stumbled across another bicycle shop, except this one was down a side street. Not only that, unlike the shop in Perth, this one was housed in what looked like an old car garage and they had painted the front of the property with huge zebra stripes. Inside the shop they sold a very specific stock of bicycles and even though it was a Sunday, they were ready and open for business and looked like they were doing incredibly well.

It was clear to me that the fundamental difference between the two businesses was simply this: the first business in Perth looked like all the other bicycle shops in the world and no doubt carried a very similar range of stock to all the others too. There seemed to be nothing discernibly different to the hundreds of competitors out there and, as a consequence, the customers ignored them and the business went under. They had unwittingly created another General Practitioner solution when the customer wants a specialist solution.

The Sydney business couldn't be more different. It's wild exterior, its funky "converted garage" interior and graffiti walls spoke to a very specific target market and solved their very particular problems in a very cool way. Not only that, it was clear from the range of stock and the kind of employees they had, that they were specialising in a particular type of bike and service for their customers and business seemed to be flourishing.

HOW TO RENOVATE YOUR BUSINESS

They were clearly the go-to experts for this kind of bike, for this target market and had deliberately created a very specific buying experience for their customers. This is a critically important point. The customer is attracted to you because they recognise immediately that you are talking to THEIR deeper needs and wants and, more importantly, because they see you as an expert in this target market. They trust you and are therefore more likely to buy from you.

Right now your customers are too busy, too stressed and too immune to marketing messages to really care about you, your product or service. Unless you position yourself to a specific target market and unless that target market can quickly see and understand your expertise in that area, your business will struggle.

Once they see you as having expertise in their needs and wants, the effort required to get the customers into your business is massively reduced.

Every day Luke or I talk to business owners who have built their businesses on what we call the "old paradigm" principles. In a nutshell the old paradigm is when you set up your business based on your core skill or strength, and then you advertise your skills to the world and hope people flock to your doorstep."

This paradigm worked well for a number of years, certainly during the 1950s, 1960s and into the early 1970s. Yet as the customer became overwhelmed with more and more advertising messages, via more and more marketing mediums (TV, the Internet and so on), the more people have tuned out and as a consequence, the less and less effective the old paradigm has become.

The new paradigm is exactly what we are outlining in this chapter. Find your red-hot niche and establish yourself as the go-to expert in that niche by solving the customers' problems better than your competitors. You solve the problems specifically by delivering your product or service in a way that makes you stand out from the crowd. Your customers then start talking about you, referring more customers and telling your marketing story to others customers on your behalf.

The old paradigm stopped working years ago and yet most business owners still attempt to market their product out to the world, rather than listening to what their target customer really wants and giving them what they want. Most companies look at Coca-Cola, Ford, Nestle and copy what they do, not realising that their industrial might was built 50, 100 or 150 years ago and even they are now beginning to market their products in a different way.

This radical approach is not simply an interesting theory; this is at the heart of exactly how Luke built his two multi-million dollar businesses and how I built successful recruitment businesses for my old bosses all around the world. It is also at the heart of the Business Renovators.

Now that you have identified your target market and you are able to communicate that your expertise, skills and strengths can solve a particular problem better than your competition, you're ready to move to the next phase of growing your business idea.

HOW TO RENOVATE YOUR BUSINESS

> **ACTION STEP**
>
> How would you describe yourself as the go-to expert to your customer (this can include the benefits of your product or service)?
>
> ....
>
> ....

STEP FOUR:
DESIGN YOUR PRODUCT OR SERVICE WITH THE CUSTOMER IN MIND

> *"Do what you do so well that they will want to see it again and bring their friends."*
> **Walt Disney**

By now you should be thinking that this is a dramatically different process to what you may have thought was the perfect way of taking your entrepreneurial idea and turning it into cash. In essence we turn the whole "corporate, institutional marketing model" on its head because it simply doesn't work anymore.

The corporate institutional marketing model went something like this:

> "I am a big company and I have a great product I want to launch to the world. I'll advertise this product everywhere and the customers will come flocking to the door."

This "model" began during the 1950s boom years and did work, primarily because advertising and mass marketing were so new and the consumer was so keen and excited to hear that marketing message. Fast-forward 60 years and the consumer is too savvy, too busy and too immune to most marketing campaigns that still follow this model.

Now here's the sad news.

Most small and medium-sized business owners have watched the "big end" of town use this model for 60 years and have simply followed them. Even today, they still continue to deliver their marketing in the very same way as they have in the past and, as a consequence, are at a loss as to why it doesn't work anymore. Nor do they understand why marketing is getting more expensive and yet getting poorer results and, most importantly, what to do to fix the problem.

The solution is in your hands.

Don't market to the mass of consumers, market to your red-hot niche market that is willing to listen to your message and try your new product or service. We have explained the process by which you identify that market. The process by which you get them to test your product or service is all about packaging it to meet their needs.

The key "gold nugget" to remember when packing your product or service is that customers think logically but they buy emotionally.

In nearly every instance, when you listen to customers post purchase they will always justify their purchases logically, yet the truth is the desire to buy is an emotional response and whatever you're packaging, you cannot underestimate the power of emotion to motivate your customer to part with their cash.

So a woman who has 10 pairs of red shoes will buy that eleventh pair and explain that she bought them because she doesn't

HOW TO RENOVATE YOUR BUSINESS

have that particular style or that size of heel in red. This is the logical reason that she uses to justify the purchase. However, the emotional trigger that may be going on for her is that these red shoes make her feel more attractive, more elegant, more at ease or happy with herself.

This is the real gold; this is what your packaging of your product or service needs to hit – the deeper emotional drivers of your customer. And it needs to do so by meeting that need and solving that problem better than your competition.

So first things first, when packaging your product or service you must be able to identify your customers' ideal shopping experience.

When I began Get Online Made Simple, all I wanted to do was make it easier for business owners to understand what they needed to do with their websites to grab more customers or make more cash. I wanted to create an online site full of easy to follow videos, so that my customers knew exactly what to do to make money online. Plus they could talk to me once every two weeks personally if they were ever stuck or frustrated.

The reason I packaged my solution like this was because I knew (after spending months talking to business owners) that they were frustrated by their lack of online knowledge yet they knew a website was important for their business growth and revenue. They hated techie jargon and they wanted to learn in a safe environment but also talk to a human being who understood their challenges and could get results for them quickly.

The second thing you must therefore do is understand the deeper emotional needs of your customer. For me specifically they were as follows:

1) Nobody likes to look like a fool, so my service was designed to ensure that people received a one-on-one service if needed, or they could learn in the comfort of their own home and make as many "mistakes" as they wanted without facing ridicule.

2) Nobody wants to be left behind. Every one of my customers knew they had to understand how to leverage the online world because that's where all of their customers and future customers were headed. So there was a deep emotional driver going on - fear of loss - and my service helped alleviate that.

As you can see, understanding the deeper emotional needs of your customer will significantly impact the way you package your product or service for your customers. As a consequence, if you get this right, your business or new business idea is going to get traction much faster.

The third and final step of the process is simply this. Based on everything you have learned about the needs of your customer (who is in your red-hot niche market) you then begin to tailor your product or service so that it directly meets those needs. As soon as you do that we believe you will begin to see the results in the cash that you generate in your business.

When Luke first started in business he was selling home computers. For many months he struggled until he came to understand the critical importance of packaging his product or service to meet the deeper needs of his customers.

Back then all home computers came in separate pieces – printers, monitors, sound cards and so on. Luke understood that most of his customers were families and very few of them had a "technical" ability with computers.

HOW TO RENOVATE YOUR BUSINESS

Understanding this, he totally rebuilt his offering to them.

He called himself the "Family PC Store", he bundled all of the parts into one complete unit so all the customer had to do was take the computer home and plug it in. In essence he made the purchasing and set-up process much easier and much less confusing. His business exploded.

On the surface level he met their "wants" by giving them a complete home computer system ready to go. He also met their deeper emotional needs. Most people don't want to look like an idiot or a fool and they found the process of buying computers confusing and sometimes downright embarrassing because the salesperson would bamboozle them with tech talk. In essence, Luke removed all of that embarrassment and met this need by packaging a remarkably simple solution and combined that with an easy process to purchase. This powerful understanding of his customer helped him create a $12 million company from an $800 start-up in less than five years.

Remember, tailor your product or services as a solution to meet exactly what your customers are asking for!

ACTION STEPS

Begin the process of identifying some of the deeper emotional needs of your customers and based on that, draw up your ideal, tailor-made service for them in detail. To help you in this process, imagine yourself as the customer enjoying your new product or service, so you are crystal clear on what you must deliver from day one.

....

....

How do your competitors package their product or service to their customers?

....

....

Write a minimum of three elements by which your product or service can beat the competitors.

....

....

....

STEP FIVE:
CREATE YOUR WORD-OF-MOUTH MEGA MARKETING MACHINE

"You will get more word-of-mouth from making people happy than anything else you could possibly do".
Andy Sernovitz

Now that you've packaged your solution it's time to get your message out there to the world and get those customers pounding on your door.

Two hundred years ago, when we lived in smaller communities before the Industrial Revolution, there was one very powerful form of marketing and advertising and it went something like this:

> **Mary** (to her next door neighbour): "Nellie, I just moved in last week and have realised my cart horse, Eric, has lost a shoe. You wouldn't happen to know a good blacksmith 'round here would you?"

HOW TO RENOVATE YOUR BUSINESS

> **Nellie**: "Well Mary (spitting on the floor), if it's a blacksmith you're after you couldn't do better than old Joe Turner. Deaf as a post he is but honest as the day is long and he's been shoeing horses in the village for 37 years. He's a good choice. There's also Will Bramble, handsome as heck but thicker than a ploughman's sandwich. He's cheaper than Joe but seems to do more work with the bigger horses so he might be your best bet."

Clearly I wanted to make you smile with that example but the message is important. What Nellie was doing back then, as did a thousand Nellies across a thousand villages, was make a word-of-mouth referral. Back in those days word-of-mouth was how you found out which merchants were good and who was not so good in your village or your local area. And back then it meant you really had to look after your customers.

Fast-forward to present day and we are right back where Nellie once stood.

The statistics show that at its very best, traditional marketing and advertising will result in about 12 per cent of your customers purchasing from you (although from personal experience I believe that figure to be on the optimistic side). However, with a word-of-mouth referral 82 per cent of customers are likely to buy from you, and if you wondered why there has been such an explosion of interest in social media, it's because social media platforms put word-of-mouth referrals on steroids.

Have you ever wondered why big companies like Nike, McDonalds, Coca-Cola, Victoria's Secret and hundreds more have leapt onto Facebook? Well, these stats will shock you.

In 2010 a company called Syncapse released a report to the public called "The Value of a Facebook Fan" and it was incredible.

Through their research they were able to see that for companies like those mentioned above, they were making more cash from customer who were ALSO fans of their Facebook page, compared to traditional customers. Here are some of their findings:

Company	Facebook Fan Spends	Traditional Customer Spends
Nokia	$171.22	$63.86
Nike	$205.02	$83.69
McDonalds	$310.18	$150.39
Coca-Cola	$190.48	$120.98

Over a period of a year some of these large organisations are making double and nearly triple the sales from customers who are also fans on Facebook, compared to more traditional customers.

For those of you who think Facebook doesn't apply to your business, if you're predominantly dealing with the general public as your customer base, then it does. What matters is what our customers think and how they act and right now they are still joining Facebook in their millions.

When Luke and I began talking about Facebook just 24 months ago, they had 650 million members. That has now risen to 845 million and growing. You need to be where your customers are and right now they are on Facebook and referring products and services – just like Nellie.

The ability to identify your target market and get them talking to you using the power of Facebook is unprecedented. Right now for every one fan of your Facebook page there are approximately 130 friends. That means for every one fan who "likes" what you do on Facebook you also have the opportunity to get your marketing message to their 130 friends.

Luke and I have 27,000-plus fans on Facebook at the time of writing this chapter. But the total number of friends of these fans is over 9,313,000. That means we can potentially market to nearly 10 million people! That is the power of Facebook and that is why Luke and I call it the Word-of-Mouth Mega Marketing Machine.

In fact, one of the greatest advantages of Facebook is that it can provide a platform to launch your idea safely and cheaply. You can build a Timeline page for your business idea (which is like a mini website homepage that sits inside Facebook) and use that to get feedback, build customers and ultimately launch your idea to the world.

HOW WE BUILT 108,000 FANS ON ONE FACEBOOK FAN PAGE IN DAYS

By far the quickest and most powerful way to build fans in Facebook and then convert them into cash-paying customers is by using Facebook's astonishing advertising platform.

The reason Facebook is such a powerful marketing tool is because, unlike any other online platform, its users share a great deal of personal information; information that allows you to generate super-targeted adverts to your customers in a very cost-effective way.

So not only can you advertise to people using the usual demographic information (age, gender, education level) you can also target people by hobbies, interests and city or town. This means if your business or business idea is based in a particular city, state or country, you can create laser-targeted adverts that will only be seen by your specific customer in your specific location. This is incredibly powerful.

Not only that but Facebook is making additional changes as we speak that will allow you to advertise in "real time" to your customer. What that means is, if a customer happens to mention a particular need in a post or update this could trigger an advert appearing on their page right at that very moment.

As Facebook continues to develop as a large corporate entity, we will no doubt see more and more exciting and astonishing opportunities for you to grow your business, your customer base and your revenue using the power of advertising on their platform.

We have had some astonishing results in the past. We've built 108,000 fans on one page in just four days, have 27,000 fans on our own business page, attracted 18,000 fans on another page in just over a week and have done so using the very same three-step formula we will share with your right now.

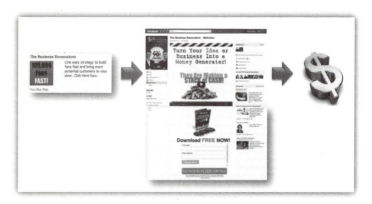

Step One: Create a compelling advert for your target market

Step Two: Take them to your conversion page and add them to your database via a compelling offer

Step Three: Once on your database, build bonding and trust via offers

HOW TO RENOVATE YOUR BUSINESS

STEP ONE: You create a compelling advert that you know will grab your customers' attention. Not only that but you ensure that advert goes only to your red-hot niche market so that you are certain they will be interested in your message and what you have to offer. Just make sure that when you run your advert you constantly test and measure it so you can see how many people have viewed the advert, how many clicked on it to visit your page and finally how many then gave you their name and email address.

Typically you should see a minimum of one to three per cent of people who click on your advert grabbing your compelling offer, although we have seen up to 12 and 15 per cent conversion rates (that means converting from passive fans into active customers).

STEP TWO: Facebook advertising allows you to decide exactly where you want to take your customers and we always take our potential customers to what we call our "Conversion Engine" page.

Our Conversion Engine page helps us achieve two fundamental outcomes. Firstly, we get the visitor (let's call her Mary), to "Like" our page. The reason we want Mary to "Like" our page is because, as we mentioned earlier, for every one person like Mary on Facebook they typically have, on average, 130 friends. As soon as Mary clicks on the "Like" button on our page, all of her friends can see she has liked our page. In essence, that means our Conversion Engine page could now be potentially viewed by a further 130 people.

To give you some idea of how staggering this viral potential is, here's a screenshot of our actual Business Renovators Fan Page. At the time, we had over 26,500 fans but in total all of those fans have 9,313,550 friends. This means we can potentially market to just under 10 million people and this is the exponential power of Facebook.

LUKE FATOOROS AND ALAN FURLONG

The second fundamental outcome we are looking to achieve for our page is to acquire the names and email addresses of our customers and here's why that is so important.

Fans can come and go but once you have a customer's email address and they are added to your database, then you have the opportunity to tell your story and market to them.

STEP THREE: It is essential to remember that the goal of any Facebook marketing strategy is to simply help you get your business or business idea marketed ethically to your red-hot niche (or target) market. As a consequence of getting your story out there you are then utilising the power of Facebook and word-of-mouth referral to build your database of customers.

Here is the GOLD.

The asset for you as an entrepreneur is not the fan page and the number of fans you have (although this is incredibly important).

The true asset for you is the number of customers on your database and how many of them purchase from you and how often. This is where the cash is made and this is where you can clearly see the results of your hard work at the front-end of the process marketing via Facebook.

So fans are fantastic but cash-paying customers who love what you do is the goal. Follow this one simple instruction and you can't go far wrong using Facebook as an incredibly powerful marketing tool for your new or established business.

STEP SIX:
CREATE A ZERO TO $100K FAST-TRACK ACTION PLAN

"Planning is bringing the future into the present so that you can do something about it now."
Alan Lakein, Author

Okay, I am certain the biggest questions you have are, "Where do I start?", "How do I get the ball rolling" and "How do I create a business that will make me $10,000 per month?"

The first thing to do is break that goal of $10,000 a month into something more achievable and here's why.

Recently I asked a business owner what her monthly goal was. She said it was to achieve a $50,000 cash profit, which is fantastic. Then I asked how long had she had had this goal and her answer was 15 years. So then I asked how often had she hit her monthly goal in 15 years and the answer was never! I took a very deep breath and explained to her that she should get rid of this goal altogether because it was not realistic; she had never achieved it and things were never going to change for her if she kept it.

Here's the truth about achieving financial success in business. Success is achieved by taking small steps forward every day; it is rarely, if ever, achieved by taking huge leaps once in a while.

So if you're reading this right now and are excited, enthusiastic and see a world of potential where you could make thousands of dollars a month, terrific, just show us how you are going to make your first $750 a month in profit.

The reason this person was so incapable of achieving her $50,000 per month goal, was because she never laid out an action plan to help her achieve her first $750 in profit and then from $750 to $1,500, and from $1,500 to $3,000, and so on. So many of us are hypnotised by the potential "big pay day" yet we never get there because that pay day is just an elusive dream without a step-by-step action plan to achieve it.

THE MOMENTUM PARADOX AND THE SECRET TO SUCCESS

The diagram below is extraordinarily powerful and explains the process of building a business and consequently why so many businesses fail.

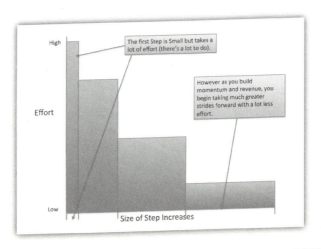

HOW TO RENOVATE YOUR BUSINESS

As you can see, when you take your first step in business there's a lot to do, a lot to learn and a lot of effort required just to take that first small step. In this case, there's a lot of effort required just to make your initial $750 per month profit. However, as you build and grow your skills, the marketing strategies you have created and the customer care systems and processes that you have put in place start doing the work for you. So, although you still need to put in effort, a lot less of that effort is required to move you onto your second step generating $1,500 a month in revenue.

Once again, as you build from $1,500 a month to $3,000 a month all of the hard work you have undertaken at the front-end of your business is now helping to propel the revenue in your business as it continues to grow.

Do you still need to put in effort? Absolutely, but nowhere near as much as you did at the start of your business or new business idea when you were getting it off the ground. This is the essence of the momentum paradox. At the start it takes a lot of effort to take a small step forward but as you go along your journey it takes less and less effort to build more and more revenue, assuming you put the right systems and structures in place to cope with that growth. If you're still doing all the work yourself as your business grows, you are not acting like a business owner but more like an employee.

So if you're a business owner and are thinking, "Hold on, this doesn't make sense to me because I'm still working hard every single day, still putting in a huge effort and only getting average revenue into my business", our response is always the same.

From day one you have operated this business in the same way people operate their jobs. If you are still working hard each and every day that tells us that there is a fundamental issue with the **structure** of your business. You should have people, systems, structures or processes doing all the hard work and not YOU. And if you reply, "But I can't afford more people, systems or structures", then we'd simply ask you to go back to your fundamentals, back to the start of this chapter and ask yourself:

- Who is my red-hot niche market and what problem do I solve for them better than my competition?
- Do my customers really know what makes my business unique and different?

If you're not clear on either of those two critical points, this may explain why you're still struggling.

WE WERE LIED TO
For the vast majority of us, our greatest influences were our parents, closely followed by our schooling, closely followed by our work environments.

The great message perpetrated in the world is that "hard work" is the key to success and like all great messages it is only partially true.

Indeed, getting a business off the ground is hard work initially, but if you are still working hard five, 10 or 15 years down the track and not making a huge amount of cash, then something is fundamentally wrong.

If your present business is not achieving what you want, here are some more questions to ask:

- Am I imposing any limitations on my business and my success?" If the answer is yes, then identify what it is you need to change.

HOW TO RENOVATE YOUR BUSINESS

- Do I need to do more sales?
- Do I need to create more joint venture partnerships?
- Do I need to get more comfortable with having a lot of money?

Now that you have reached this far into the chapter you will have realised that there are some core fundamental actions you must take. Each action will help you take that next step to hitting your first monthly revenue goal. The good news is that unlike the majority of people who give up at the first step because all they see is a lot of hard work, you can now see that this is a natural part of the process of building a successful business and the workload will decrease as your revenue increases (the Momentum Paradox).

So it is time to look at building your business or new business idea even if you have limited money, limited resources, limited experience and want to keep your overheads to a minimum. It is now time to take action.

So no more reading, no more sitting back. It is time you looked at all of the action items thus far in this chapter and began to write them down in priority order. What must you do first? Is it research into niche markets, based on your skills and abilities to generate a "cash-creating" idea? Do you need to go back and look at the fundamentals of your present business and ask yourself the tough questions about your target market and in fact, whether you actually have one?

The structure is here, all you need to do is start taking action.

ACTION STEPS

What are my top three priorities to help me make an additional (or new) $750 per month in profit?

....

....

....

Design a weekly breakdown of activity that will result in sales.

....

....

....

Identify a minimum of two joint venture partners.

....

....

Think of at least one complimentary product or service you could add to your solution from a joint venture partner, so you can increase sales immediately with zero additional expense.

....

....

HOW TO RENOVATE YOUR BUSINESS

STEP SEVEN:
YOUR FREEDOM DAY

"One of the deep secrets of life is that all that is really worth doing is what we do for others".
Lewis Carol

It is time to take control of your own destiny so let me ask you another question. What does freedom mean to you?

If you cannot define it, you will never achieve it. So let's get started and get really clear on your personal definition of freedom because life is too precious to spend it chasing the next money goal and the next money goal simply for the sake of money.

Having an "ultimate outcome" is key to ensuring you don't get trapped by your ego and spend the rest of your life creating an ever expanding empire, yet never taking the time out to enjoy the freedom your money can provide.

Achieving freedom is a series of steps.

The first step is to achieve financial independence. That means you can cover all of your expenses (mortgage payments, bills, living expenses, holiday expenses, spending money) with passive cashflow from your businesses.

In essence, the revenue of your businesses is creating profits and income. That income allows you to live life on your terms without worrying about the bills. Not only that, because you're creating profits your businesses have a real value. That value helps you create "wealth" because now you have a real cash-creating asset that also has intrinsic value in its own right. That wealth can be tapped into by selling some, or all, of your company and receiving a significant lump sum in the process.

The second step in achieving freedom is what we call hitting the "10-year Target".

What that means is if you were to stop everything today, you would have enough cash in the bank to live (at present levels) very comfortably for the next 10 years. The beauty about this second level is that you are able to achieve "peace of mind". You know that even if the absolute worst was to happen, you could survive comfortably for a decade and use that time to begin growing your next income streams based on everything that you have learned from your journey thus far.

Henry Ford once said that the reason he was at "peace" was not because of his extraordinary wealth but because, he said, if he lost it all tomorrow, he had the skills, knowledge and experience to make it back any time he wanted.

The third and final step is financial freedom. This is the point where you have enough cash and cash-producing assets in your life so that you never have to worry about money for the rest of your life. At this point you can decide what you do with all of your time and all of your freedom.

The big question is what does freedom mean to you?

How much exactly would you need in your bank account to live comfortably? How much income would you need per year and per month to be happy? If it is $150,000-a-year in income, that equates to a $12,500-a-month revenue pipeline that you must create. Therefore, how many assets would you need to have in your life to provide that freedom, or how much cash in the bank would you need for the rest of your life to ensure you were truly free?

HOW TO RENOVATE YOUR BUSINESS

Next, what would you do with your time and freedom? Who would you spend it with?

It is important that you have a clear idea of how you would live your life, knowing that money was no longer an issue. Without that clarity it would be easy to be swallowed up by the process of making money and forget completely why you started out on the journey in the first place. The truth is you can't take the stuff with you; the only thing that is really precious is your TIME. This is certainly a limited resource and you don't want to get to the end of your life amassing a fortune and realise you never really lived fully.

The money, at the end of the day, is only a vehicle to get your time back and your freedom back and Luke and I strongly believe that all of that extra time and freedom will inevitably bring you to the point of asking...

"What is the purpose of my life?"

So many people struggle financially all of their lives and as a consequence, never have the freedom to do what they truly wish to do. They never have the opportunity or the time to enjoy life to the fullest, have incredible experiences or give back and make a contribution to the communities that need it most. The great gift of their life is squandered in a never ending struggle to make ends meet, that only gets worse for most people after retirement, not better.

There is something fundamentally wrong with our society, or any society that creates such misery. We live in an era where debt and the servicing of debt has ensured that the majority of our citizens are living in fear of losing everything, are up to their eyeballs in stress just trying to keep their heads above water or are working hard in jobs they hate because they feel they have no alternative.

Well, there is an alternative and we have just presented it to you in this incredibly powerful chapter. It is really over to you now.

You can read this book, agree on a few points, agree that you've learnt a few things and maybe even write down a couple of actions items. If that is all you do, then truly, we have wasted your time.

Unless you now take some action, come and see us live, go out and begin doing your research, start changing elements within your business or begin taking steps to start your business by identifying your red-hot niche market, you will see no results. All you need is the courage to take that one first, small step to change your life.

As Johann Wolfgang Von Goethe once said:

> *"Until one is committed, there is hesitancy, the chance to draw back. Concerning all acts of initiative (and creation), there is one elementary truth that ignorance of which kills countless ideas and splendid plans: that the moment one definitely commits oneself, then Providence moves too.*
>
> *All sorts of things occur to help one that would never otherwise have occurred. A whole stream of events issues from the decision, raising in one's favor all manner of unforeseen incidents and meetings and material assistance, which no man could have dreamed would have come his way.*
>
> *Whatever you can do, or dream you can do, begin it.*
>
> *Boldness has genius, power, and magic in it.*
>
> *Begin it now."*

HOW TO RENOVATE YOUR BUSINESS

ACTION STEPS

Do your maths. How much in total will it cost to get your new business idea off the ground?

....

....

....

Do a full personal expenses breakdown. How much do you spend each month in total (this will provide your first indication of how much cash you need to create to achieve financial independence).

....

....

....

Review both sets of figures and set a "go live" date for your new business, or new business idea.

....

Build your safety bridge. What do you do if you get stuck? Do you have a mentor, coach or guide you can talk to who has successfully navigated their way through this process?

....

....

....

CONCLUSION

If you hoped there was a genuine "Get Rich Quick" opportunity out there, then we promise you there is no such thing. Building long-term, sustainable wealth is like building a house and it begins with solid foundations.

The process we have outlined in this chapter is revolutionary, it's challenging and it's unique. It is based on our combined 45 years of sales, marketing and business-building experience, so it is not a "clever theory"; it is a path, a journey and a process of financial and personal growth that is exciting, challenging and available to anyone who simply has the courage to step forward.

Luke and I invite you right now to take that step and join us on one of the most exhilarating journeys of your life.

How would it feel to know that you have the skills and the abilities to create wealth by solving other people's problems? By creating a business that you feel reflects you and your personal values?

How would it feel to never have to worry about the bills anymore or, more importantly, to be able just to hang out with the family on a weekday just because you can?

How would it feel to never have to set an alarm clock anymore, or work for a boss you don't respect, or do a commute that kills your soul piece by piece, each and every day?

We know how it feels to be there and now we are committed to getting others to move from that point and join us on this astonishing journey. We encourage you to join us so you can experience life as it is meant to be for you, not how it has been forced upon you. Thank you for your time with us. We wish you the very best and hope to meet you soon.

Chapter 3
REAL ESTATE RESCUES

"These days, smart investors are making their money in real estate when they buy."

DOMINIQUE GRUBISA

PROFILE

DOMINIQUE GRUBISA

Dominique Grubisa is a property developer and investor, an entrepreneur, published author, speaker and practising barrister with over 20 years' legal experience.

She has become the "go-to" guru for all matters legal and commercial in Australia, and has been widely featured in print media, radio and on national television.

Dominique has developed new techniques and strategies which have helped thousands to not just survive but thrive in these unique economic times.

REAL ESTATE RESCUES

HOW TO PROFIT IN REAL ESTATE IN THE NEW ECONOMY: A CRASH COURSE IN PRE-FORECLOSURE AND SHORT SALES

Congratulations! You have taken an important step in securing your financial future, and I'm honoured that you decided to take it with me. I bought my first distressed property at the age of 26 – and it was actually by mistake! I didn't know what I was doing, and had no training or experience in property investing (I thought it was something they did in America which we could not do here in Australia). At that time, there was no such thing. I just happened to be in the right place at the right time and the deal of the decade fell across my lap.

When I went to buy my next property, of course I wanted to find the same thing again – a distressed vendor with the bank breathing down their neck - but to my dismay, no one ever advertised this sort of deal and the few "deceased estate" or "mortgagee" sales I found advertised were already out there and every Tom, Dick and Harry were buzzing around them in a lather – pushing the price up beyond my reach.

They say that necessity is the mother of invention. I wanted to find the best deals before they even came on the market and to have "inside" information that other investors were not privy to. I found a way to do this in Australia and for the first time ever I am sharing it with those entrepreneurs who are ready, in the words of famous investor, Warren Buffet to be:

> *"...fearful when others are greedy and
> greedy when others are fearful."*

Just as there are very few classes to teach our children about credit and how to manage their finances, no one has ever set up a curriculum to teach you the ropes of evaluating, investing in, and managing distressed real estate purchases. I do not even promise that here. You will actually only really learn by doing. The goal here is to shorten the learning curve for you. Right now, the entire foreclosure, mortgagee repossession and bankruptcy process may seem quite foreign, and even a bit secretive, but once you get into it, you'll find that it's actually quite simple!

People buy a home, then, for any number of reasons they cannot afford to keep it or need to sell it quickly. They either market it and are very motivated to take a low price in return for a quick sale, or if they don't pull this off, the lender or trustee in bankruptcy takes the home off them and sells it. Pretty simple. Although there are certainly a few more steps in between, that outline pretty much sums up the situation. The trick is learning how to make money between the steps. In this next section, I'll take you through a crash course on the recovery of distressed asset process to help you start to identify where the real opportunities lie.

WHAT ARE FORECLOSURES AND MORTGAGEE REPOSSESSIONS?

The first thing you need is a clear understanding of what foreclosure and mortgagee repossessions are. When you mention the word foreclosure or a mortgagee sale, most people think of unfortunate people who got in over their heads and lost their property to the bank.

This is only partially accurate. While there is certainly an element of truth in the statement, the concept of foreclosures is actually

REAL ESTATE RESCUES

bigger than that. There are many reasons why properties go through foreclosure, and it involves an entire process whose pieces can be broken down into three basic phases – pre-foreclosure, short sale and mortgagee sale.

WHAT ARE PRE-FORECLOSURES?

As you will soon see, this is where the "real" money is made. I have purchased properties in all different steps in the process, but it is during this pre-foreclosure phase where your efforts will yield the greatest reward.

Pre-foreclosure, simply defined, is the time period between where a homeowner misses his or her first mortgage payment, and the date when the bank commences legal proceedings to repossess the property.

You will note that I am using two expressions here: "foreclosure" and "mortgagee repossession". The two are interchangeable here for all intents and purposes however, at law the distinction is that with a foreclosure, the lender goes through the legal process of getting the lender off the title to the property and putting themselves on the deeds as the owner of the property but with a mortgagee repossession, the lender just gets a court order to take over the property and sell it but the owner is still on the title deeds. In reality lenders do not bother to "foreclose" and get themselves on the title; they take the property as a mortgagee in possession and try and sell it as expediently as possible whilst still achieving the highest possible market price (by law they cannot undersell the property or even advertise it as a mortgagee or fire sale).

WHAT ARE SHORT SALES?

During the foreclosure or repossession process, the lender will always lose money. Sometimes a great deal of it. With the advent of creative mortgages over the past several years, combined with a cycle of soft or declining real estate markets, some homeowners actually become "upside down" on their property, that is to say, they can't afford to sell as they owe the lender more than what the property will sell for. By the time they pay a real estate agent's sales commission, all the costs and fees, as well as the debts associated with the property, they actually end up owing the lender money in order to sell their home. At the moment in Australia one in five properties in Queensland and Western Australia is upside down or "under water".

In these circumstances, many homeowners and lenders are faced with the difficult choice of the lesser of two evils. Can they trade through things until the market turns or should they sell up now and cut their losses?

The short sale is where the lender agrees to accept full payment for the mortgage debt in an amount that is less than the homeowner actually owes. Most homeowners don't know that this is even possible, and they certainly don't know how to structure a short sale transaction. When the circumstances are right, you'll be in a position to help.

STEPS IN THE FORECLOSURE OR MORTGAGEE REPOSSESSION PROCESS

Most people believe that the foreclosure process starts when the lender sues the borrower in a court of law. In reality, it starts way before that. It starts as soon as the homeowner misses a payment.

In a typical foreclosure process, there are actually 12 steps. So you understand all the differences, and how to determine where the homeowner is in the progression, let's take a quick look at each one.

REAL ESTATE RESCUES

1) **The missed payment:** For a variety of reasons, the payment is missed, and once a borrower gets behind, it is difficult to catch back up.

2) **The payment reminder:** Hoping that it's just an oversight, the lender will send a gentle reminder to the borrower within the first 10 to 25 days.

3) **No response:** If the payment still hasn't found its way to the lender, there will be a series of more strongly worded letters, followed by a few phone calls to the homeowner to find out what's wrong.

4) **Collection:** If the lender and homeowner have not reached a resolution to enable the payment to be caught up, usually by the 60th day delinquency, the lender will turn the matter over to its internal collection department, or its loss mitigation department.

5) **Work out:** If the lender can talk to the homeowner (the homeowner is probably getting really skilled at dodging phone calls), they will try and agree on a "work out", or loan modification to get the borrower back on track. This can include partial payments for a short period of time, payments added to the end of the loan, or any other of several scenarios based on the borrower's situation. This is a mandatory step for most loans and can work very well if the borrower can demonstrate that his/her circumstances are only temporary.

6) **Outside collection:** The homeowner has now missed three payments, the lender knows that the problem is serious, and the likelihood of the homeowner catching up is slim. The repayment is now 90 days past due and the matter is

usually referred to outside lawyers to begin legal proceedings against the homeowner. They aren't typically as nice as the lender's own employees.

7) **The Notice of Default:** If the borrower has still not brought arrears up to date on the loan or made an arrangement with the lender to do so, a notice of default will be sent via ordinary mail to the borrower (this is a legal requirement; it is a formal notice required under statute to be sent in each state).

8) **Statement of Claim:** If the amount owing is still outstanding the lender will file court proceedings against the borrower seeking orders for judgment on the full amount owing on the loan, repossession of the property, interest and legal costs.

9) **Judgment for Possession:** A judge will order the homeowner to hand over possession of the property to the lender.

10) **Sheriff's Order:** The sheriff gives the borrower notice that officers will be attending to change the locks – the notice will nominate a time and a day and the homeowner will need to leave the property vacant by this time.

11) **Auction day:** If the homeowner has not somehow gotten his/her act together, the property is auctioned off to the highest bidder; all is liquidated to pay off the lender. This is usually an anticlimactic event, except for the homeowner. This is the day he or she really starts to lose the property. If the property is passed in at auction, the lender keeps trying to sell it.

REAL ESTATE RESCUES

12) **The new owner moves in:** Once the property has been secured, the new owner or investor can fully take over and they settle on the purchase, paying out the lender.

THE BEST MARKET IS NOW

In the past two years, foreclosures have increased in every state in the country. We look at some of the many reasons for this in a moment, but it is a trend that is likely to continue for several years. As a result, the opportunities for investors have never been better.

Real estate in general works in cycles. There are good years, and some not so good years, but overall, values will eventually increase. This has been the case for well over 100 years. But foreclosure cycles operate differently. Although some cycles are driven by real estate values, there are other factors that drive them as well, such as a major industry closing down, an increase in the cost of living or a generally flat economy. Interest rate spikes or major tax increases can also affect foreclosure rates.

But for the investor, the best market and the best time to get started is now. Foreclosures happen every day, and regardless of your level of experience, or the present market conditions, I can teach you how to effectively evaluate each opportunity and pick the right one. They exist in every city, in every state, in every market condition. But to fully appreciate how the markets play into your hands, let's look at the reasons why the number of foreclosures has increased all of a sudden.

REASONS FORECLOSURES ARE INCREASING

The biggest reason foreclosures keep increasing is that Australians can't seem to live on what they earn. They keep borrowing money for toys (boats, cars, resort holidays etc) that they can't afford, don't need, and can't pay for. Credit card debt keeps spiralling upward every year, and the homes people purchase (thanks to creative mortgage products that they don't understand) can leave them one pay cheque away from disaster in every direction.

1) **No and Low Doc Loans:** Creative programs that require little or no down payment, interest-only type loan payments, or stated income (what I call " liar loans") have led people down a path of destruction. Many of these loans were predicated on the fact that property values would continue to rise and when they didn't, the walls came crashing down. As I write this, more than one out of every 10 no or low doc loans are in default around the country.

2) **Weak economic conditions:** A shift of many jobs off-shore to Asia coupled with poor retail figures and a strong Australian dollar, has seen employment loss cripple entire Australian communities. Cities that were reliant on the success of just one or two main industries have had a hard time competing with the new job sectors, and the result has been an increase in foreclosure activity. I know that we have mining in our two speed economy but our retail, manufacturing and building sectors are really doing it tough.

3) **Predatory lending practices:** Creditors advertise low rates and easy payment terms. They come in to steal the equity of elderly and unsophisticated borrowers with programs that are so onerous, there is no way the homeowner is going to be able to make the payments. It may be for home repairs or a refinance transaction that promises a lot of cash in hand that's too tempting for people to pass up. It amounts to theft of their equity as they treat their home loan as a big ATM, drawing out the money to meet loan repayments from a line of credit secured against the home (as they have inadequate income to service the debt). In the end, interest rates go

up, payments become higher than the homeowner's entire monthly income, and the inevitable result is foreclosure.

4) **Low interest rates:** This has been a big one over the past few years: low "teaser" rates that sound attractive – until you find out how high and how quickly they can adjust. Low market rates have made access to credit extremely easy in the immediate aftermath of the Global Financial Crisis (GFC). Add to that the government stimulus packages and first homebuyer grants which lured unsuspecting homeowners in with attractive packages at the time. Unfortunately, even a slight bump in interest rates or one hiccup in their income results in hard times for the family.

5) **Over-extended first-time homeowners:** With the government's blessing, and lenders as willing accomplices, first-time ownership rates have skyrocketed to an all-time high. New government programs and a flood of first-time homebuyer incentives have made the Australian dream turn into a nightmare for those unprepared. This miscalculating the upkeep on a home, budgeting responsibilities, and increased consumer pricing on goods and services, combined with a low initial deposit payment, have left people on the edge.

6) **Higher Loan-to-Value and Debt-to-Income Ratios:** Twenty years ago, it was common for a homeowner to need at least 20 per cent initial deposit to buy a home. Lenders also required that borrowers not spend more than 28 per cent of their monthly income when their monthly debts were added in. Loan-to-value percentages have shot up dramatically, to the point that very few borrowers actually have 20 per cent initial payment necessary to avoid mortgage insurance. In addition, automated underwriting practices and sub-prime

mortgages have allowed income ratios to fly past 36 per cent, to 50 per cent, 60 per cent or even 70 per cent in some cases. There just isn't enough income at the end of the month for homeowners to make mortgage repayments.

7) **Artificial values:** As the economy hummed along, and real estate became increasingly easier to obtain, the natural evolution was for values to go up. It's a simple case of supply and demand. As the number of "qualified borrowers" increased, demand went up and prices grew. They grew so fast in some areas of the country, that double-digit appreciation was considered the norm.

Homeowners treated their homes as automatic teller machines, and as values continued to increase, eventually the incomes of would-be homeowners could not support the payments, and the "bubble" exploded.

Property speculation and artificial values were most prevalent in Queensland and Western Australia – so prices in these areas have been hardest hit in the recent downturn. It is in these areas that lenders engaged in the riskiest lending practices and borrowers in the most rampant speculation. There is a reason why these are also the areas with the highest foreclosure rates.

Some states were hurt worse than others, but we are all feeling it in one way or another. This has left unsuspecting homeowners with artificially inflated property prices in a position whereby they can't refinance and can't sell. Their only choice left is to go down with the ship – the foreclosure route. Well that is until now – you guys will have another solution for these people.

REAL ESTATE RESCUES

FORECLOSURES AND SHORT SALES – NEITHER ILLEGAL NOR UNETHICAL

Yes, there are people you will meet who are in dire situations. You will be tested emotionally, and hear some heartbreaking stories. You did not cause it, nor can you necessarily fix it. And you don't need to take advantage of it to make a profit. When you are negotiating free foreclosure transactions, you should never feel guilty about what you are doing. If you don't help out the homeowner, someone else will and that someone else may try and take advantage of the situation. Worse still, if no one intervenes the bank will cause untold damage and heartache for them for many months to come. You are their knight in shining armour.

Many investors will become drawn into a situation and will be tempted to take advantage of sellers. These are small-minded people with a scarcity mentality who like to create a win/lose deal. Don't do it; it will end your career quickly.

Always try to help the homeowner. You are providing a service and should not feel any guilt about doing a deal. In most cases, the bank will end up taking the property back anyway, and you are providing a way for the homeowner to save some face, maybe their credit rating, and definitely additional heartache. You are saving the bank time and money, and you expect to get paid for your knowledge and experience in solving a problem you did not create. Nothing I ever suggest or teach in any way should be construed or used for illegal or unethical practices. Do it the right way, and you will build a great reputation and help a lot of people who have their backs to the wall.

WHAT YOU NEED FOR SUCCESS

So what do you need to make this process a success and start building a personal real estate fortune? Well, here's my short list for starters:

1) Knowledge or at least the ability to learn

2) Great organisational skills

3) Cash or at least access to people with cash

4) Patience and good listening skills

5) The ability and love of talking to and dealing with people

6) Lots of persistence.

If you start with these, the rest will fall into place. A lot of people get tripped up on item three. Yes, it is a lot easier if you have stacks of cash lying around, and a credit report that's glowing and the ability to borrow a tonne of money for whatever you want. If that's you, you can get started a lot faster, but then you'll just need a "bird dog" hunting will to go out and find pre-foreclosure properties to simply invest your cash in.

In assuming that most of you do not fit directly into that category, I do want to take a moment and be brutally honest with you. If you are expecting to do no work and just have money roll in, that won't be the case; you will get out what you put in with this system but it will not be like pressing a magic button where everything will happen – you will have to do the work. Another piece of advice for those of you "Type A" personalities like me, you'll get excited as you read through these materials but don't go out and quit your day job, at least not right away.

If you can do what is hard, life will be easy but it is not instant money and you should not put this kind of pressure on yourself.

16 STEPS TO SUCCESS
I have developed a concise 16-step process for successful investing in distressed property.

REAL ESTATE RESCUES

Step 1: Locate the property. Find distressed properties and motivated vendors. Divorces, deceased estates, bankruptcies and properties that are heading into foreclosure are a great place to start.

Step 2: Contact the owner and arrange a meeting.

Step 3: Verify the initial information given to you by the homeowner.

Step 4: Conduct an investigation, also known as doing your homework!

Step 5: Inspect the property.

Step 6: Calculate the value of your investment. You will never pay retail again using this system.

Step 7: Analyse your costs and profits. None of this makes any sense unless you can make a profit.

Step 8: Negotiate with the owner.

Step 9: Negotiate with lenders.

Step 10: Negotiate with lawyers. Lawyers may well be involved in the transaction, so you will need to talk to the right people, and get the wrong ones out of the way.

Step 11: Negotiate a short sale. Times are tough and lenders are in a dealing mood. You will need to set up, check, and structure a short sale for the homeowner and present it to get lender approval.

Step 12: Negotiate the purchase. Nothing happens until the owner agrees to sell the property to you.

Step 13: Protect your interest. Once the deal is set, you will need to know how to protect your new property and avoid last-minute surprises.

Step 14: Fix it up. There will be repairs, sometimes lots of repairs!

Step 15: Sell or rent it. It's only fun if you make a profit so we will look at the specifics of making sure that you make money on your investment.

Step 16: Do it again! If you've followed the steps correctly, you'll be excited to try again. Each deal is different, and a fortune is waiting right around the corner.

THREE PHASES OF FORECLOSURE

There are three stages of foreclosure. You will quickly learn how to recognise which phase the property you are looking at is at.

1) **Pre-foreclosure stage**: This is the period between when a homeowner misses a payment, and when the lender commences legal action.

2) **Short sale**: This is where a deal can be cut with the lender to pay out the loan on the property for less than what is owed on it.

3) **Mortgagee sale**: This is where the lender sells the property.

The first phase is where we will be locating our properties in the first instance – we can then follow them down the foreclosure path whilst trying to acquire the property during each phase. The earlier you get to a deal the better your chances of paying a good price for the property. During the public auction stage, there has been more attention brought to the property as by then it has been actively marketed, and the owners have been "beaten up" and are worn out. Buying at this stage may be both risky and competitive.

Are there deals out there? Yes, but they take a lot of work, and luck to get. Properties that are purchased from the lender via a mortgagee sale will almost always be bought at auction. First, almost all properties are listed with real estate agents, and at fair market prices. That makes it a little hard to make a profit. Due to the recent rash of foreclosures, you may come upon advertised "mortgagee auctions". Good deals can be found, but there are many pros at these things, and you're likely to end up over-bidding.

Banks are required to market repossessed properties through public auction by law, and to try to get the highest possible retail value for the asset. At this point, the property may have already been fixed up, and the lender has taken their loss. They are under no pressure to wheel and deal, and most properties end up selling for within 10 per cent of the asking price.

EVERYTHING YOU NEED TO KNOW ABOUT THE FORECLOSURE PROCESS

Now let's get down to terms and details of the foreclosure process that you need to know. This section helps you get a handle on the players, documents and clauses, and exactly what happens along the way.

Security instruments: When a loan is made, either residential or commercial, the property is put up as collateral to secure repayment. This security instrument is better known as a "mortgage". A mortgage involves two parties: a mortgagee who is the lender and a mortgagor who is the borrower. The borrower (mortgagor) signs a loan agreement and a mortgage, which is held by the lender (mortgagee) until the loan is paid off.

Two types of lenders: Real estate loans, secured by a mortgage, are provided by two types of lenders:

1) Institutional lenders, or

2) Private lenders.

Institutional lenders include banks, mortgage lenders, mortgage bankers, credit unions, capital real estate investment trusts and insurance companies.

Private lenders include everyone else - individuals, businesses, private companies, associations or investment groups. You need to recognise what type of lender you are dealing with because that will have a direct effect on how you approach the deal.

Mortgage lender versus mortgage broker: When dealing with mortgage entities, you want to get to decision-makers. It helps to understand the roles of the two types of mortgage:

1) A mortgage lender is a licensed entity who has its own funds or access to funds to directly lend to a borrower.

2) A mortgage broker is a licensed individual or company who is committed to initiate loan applications and represent the programs of many different mortgage lenders to borrowers. Mortgage brokers earn a fee directly from the lender or the borrower, or a combination of the two.

Even though a mortgage broker may have initiated the original loan for the borrower, they will not be of any help in negotiating or tracking down the current loan information.

HOW THE FORECLOSURE PROCESS IS STOPPED

It is important to understand how the foreclosure process is stopped. There are several ways a borrower or lender can stop

REAL ESTATE RESCUES

or stall the entire sequence of events, which could affect your timing on a purchase of the property:

- **Reinstatement:** The borrower can pay back any delinquent amounts at any time prior to judgment (and sometimes even after if the lender agrees) and reinstate the loan.

- **Forbearance:** The lender and borrower could enter into what's called a forbearance agreement, which allows the borrower additional time to bring the loan current or make other payment arrangements.

- **Bankruptcy:** If the borrower filed for bankruptcy at any time prior to judgment for possession being made, the process crunches to a halt whilst a trustee in bankruptcy takes over the homeowner's financial affairs.

- **Note modification:** The lender has the right to alter the terms in the notice to make it easier for the borrower to make the payments. While the borrower has to agree to the terms, such modifications are becoming more common with the drastic increase in foreclosures. The lender can alter the interest rate, payment amount, terms, and may even convert a variable rate loan to a fixed rate loan to keep the borrower in the home.

- **Short pay:** Different from a short sale, a short pay allows the borrower to pay off the lender for less than is owed, but they remain in the property. Usually done in refinance situations, this is still cheaper for the lender than a full-blown foreclosure, but is rare because it's hard for the borrower to qualify for any type of refinance any more (once they've defaulted on a mortgage).

- **Prepayment plan:** Similar to a note modification, the lender and borrower agree to a new payment plan without altering the terms of the loan. This is a great option for the lender because the foreclosure option is still readily available if the borrower doesn't follow through on the new payment schedule. This is the most common initial option, and can involve payments added to the end of the loan, bi-weekly payments, or other altered payments for a period of time until the borrower gets back on their feet.

- **Deed in lieu of foreclosure:** Here they simply sign over the deed to the lender without having to go through the drawn out foreclosure process. If the homeowner really doesn't want the property, this saves time and aggravation for everyone involved.

EVERYTHING YOU NEED TO KNOW ABOUT FORECLOSURE PROPERTIES

Once a homeowner is "upside down" in their home mortgage, there is an opportunity to use this to your advantage while helping them out of a tough situation. Everybody wins!

Temporary market fluctuations, life situations, and just bad stuff can force homeowners to sell their properties through a short sale to avoid foreclosure. Most investors, and even homeowners, walk away from these situations, but this is where all your work in locating these properties and your knowledge of the process can bring you big rewards that are well worth your efforts.

Short sales occur every day, but few people know how to negotiate one, let alone how to profit from one.

Here's a simple rule that you as an investor should abide by: if the owner has less than 15 per cent equity in the property, we look at short sale opportunities. More than 15 per cent, we

REAL ESTATE RESCUES

are buying the equity. In this section, let's focus on the short sale transaction, find out who is involved, and how to get the deal done.

WHAT DOES "UPSIDE DOWN" MEAN?

The basic Australian dream of owning a home is still alive and strong, albeit a little sickly lately. We all want the very best we can afford and to improve our lifestyle over time. Many homeowners have purchased a home that really was at their affordability limit, or even beyond it. They were able to do this using creative lending products that may not have been in their best interests.

Many homeowners refinance to remove equity from their homes to make improvements or to finance other purchases. Now they find that their total loan balance far exceeds the current appraised value of their home. When you can't sell it for enough to cover the amount owed on the home, you are "upside down". In other words your head is under financial water.

UNDERSTANDING A SHORT SALE AND A SHORT PAY

When a lender releases a homeowner from their mortgage at anything less than the full amount owed, they are accepting an amount "short" of the agreed-on pay-out figure. The costs to legally repossess a home can be quite high, with estimates starting at $50,000 on average for the lender. It's not hard to see that the lender might be willing to accept something short of the entire mortgage balance in order to get out of the situation. In a short sale, the homeowner is basically paying a smaller percentage on each dollar owed.

If the lender proceeds to a mortgagee repossession, it is a legal action, and the time necessary to carry it to completion can be months to more than a year. When the mortgagee sale is over, if the amount received doesn't cover the mortgage, fees, and costs, the lender can file a deficiency judgment against the borrower for the difference.

The problem with deficiency judgements is that they are a legal claim on the money, with no indication that they'll actually receive it. Further collection actions must be taken, and those can cost the lender even more money. Another drawback is that the lender usually has reserve requirements for non-performing loans. They must maintain liquid funds to cover the shortfall. These funds cannot be reinvested or used to generate income. As you can imagine, this isn't a fun position for the lender.

As a result, you can see why a lender might agree to a sale to a qualified buyer for an amount short of the mortgage owed by the homeowner.

In a short sale, there is a third-party buyer who is willing to purchase the property at an amount that will not satisfy the balance of the loan. The lender may be willing to allow this because the cost and time involved to repossess the home would cost them more than the shortfall, and they aren't certain to receive more at a mortgagee sale or auction. They will also avoid the requirements for holding reserves during the foreclosure process. A successful short sale requires that all parties involved see that it is in their best interests, in other words, everybody wins.

THE FOUR PARTIES INVOLVED
There are actually four parties involved in a short sale transaction. They are:

1) **Property owner:** Though their credit score is usually impacted the same in terms of ability to refinance with a short sale as with a mortgagee sale, most lenders will settle

up without entering a default on a borrower's credit report. As an investor, this gives you some extra ammunition to motivate the seller into a transaction. They need to look past the current situation and start to think about how to rebuild their financial life (although it may be hard).

2) **Investor who owns the loan:** Loans are bought and sold in packages in the financial market. The investors who own these loans could be a pension fund or a bank. Banks and financial institutions are regulated, and those reserve issues come into play when they have loans that are underperforming. Pension funds and private groups who purchase mortgages also have incentives to get bad loans off the books. They will also have to agree to the short sale.

3) **Servicer who is servicing the loan:** This is the business or entity who is handling the collection and disbursal of mortgage payments. Whether they were paid up front, or with ongoing transaction fees, or both, the loan servicer is not interested in continuing to try to collect payments from a borrower unable to make them. They will be the main party you deal with, but cannot individually sign off on a short sale.

4) **Purchaser buying the property:** This could be you, an investor looking for a great deal on a home purchased below the true value, or maybe it's a home in which you want to live. Either way, buying a home at a short sale can result in instant equity if you understand the process and work through it properly.

WHO TO TALK TO

One of the first questions is: who do you talk to? Homeowners will not have a clue where to start (or may not even know a short sale is possible) and most real estate agents don't have the expertise or they wait until it's too late. You need to get started early. Consider these questions:

- Who processes short sale requests? The servicer (not necessarily the same party as the end lender) is who you need to contact about the possibility of a short sale. They will coordinate the decision as to whether they (including the end investor) want to allow it, and how much of a shortfall they are willing to take.

- Why don't lenders want to do it? It's a last resort. Just as the homeowner has made a promise to pay his or her mortgage, the lender has made promises to investors as to the likely return on funds invested in mortgages. Settling for an amount short of the expected return is damaging to their credibility with investors, causing formal and informal negative effects on their ability to gather future funds for new mortgages. You've got to show them why a short sale is the best option.

- Can the borrower pass a hardship test? The borrower must prove to the lender that they are truly in a hardship situation that makes it impossible to follow through on their mortgage payment commitments. Because the lender is going to take a negative hit for a short sale, they want to be certain that there is no alternative.

- Who makes the final decision? The money for this loan came from an investor. This investor put up the funds with an expectation of a certain return, and s/he will make the decision as to whether the short sale is in his/her best interests or not.

- Who do I contact first? Start with a loss mitigation department where the borrower is making their payments. Do not talk to the customer service people, you will get nowhere fast. Tell them you are preparing a written proposal to purchase the subject property and get a contact name, phone number, and email address for them.

STEPS IN A SHORT SALE TRANSACTION

Before you undertake the process of short sale negotiations with the lender, it is critical you understand the steps in the process, who is responsible for what, and what documentation will be needed to get the lender's acceptance. These 11 steps will be necessary to get a successful short sale approved and to the closing table:

1) **Situation analysis:** After evaluating the value and condition of the property and the outstanding balance on the loan, it is determined that the property is upside down and a sale would not pay off the lender.

2) **Get permission:** You will need to obtain a signed borrower authorisation (see page 123) to make contact with the lender. They won't speak to you without it.

3) **Contact lender:** Contact the loss mitigation department or the person listed on the letter from the lender to the homeowner. Try to make initial contact while the borrower is right there; it is easier in case the lender wants to receive verbal authorisation as well.

4) **Write hardship letter:** The borrower will have to write a detailed letter regarding his or her situation. It must include compelling reasons for the lender to do a short sale, and that the alternative is foreclosure or bankruptcy.

5) **Get repair estimates:** Get three estimates from licensed contractors as to the costs to bring the property to marketable condition.

6) **Supporting documentation:** Put together supporting documents to prove the hardship and paint the picture for the lender. These include financial statements, payslips, bank statements, tax returns, credit reports, medical bills, divorce decree, and so on.

7) **Purchase agreement:** The next step is to agree with the homeowner as to the purchase price and pay-off amounts to the lender. The borrower should get zero, or the lender will not go along with a short sale.

8) **Submit package:** Submit the short sale package to the lender demonstrating that this is the best solution for the lender (see checklist below for what to include).

9) **Lender evaluation:** Lender will get a price opinion, which is similar to a drive-by appraisal to support value and situation.

10) **Negotiate with lender:** You may go back and forth a couple of times. Develop rapport with the loss mitigation specialist, but they will need to get approval from the servicer of the loan as well.

11) **Close the deal:** Lender will issue an approval letter to accept the short pay off. Close the deal.

SHORT SALE PACKAGE CHECKLIST

The presentation of the package to the lender is one of the key factors in getting your short sale approved. The following are items that should be included in the package to a lender (in order):

REAL ESTATE RESCUES

1) Cover letter proposal from investor

2) Borrower hardship letter

3) Borrower supporting documentation:
   a. Credit report
   b. Financial statement
   c. Payslips
   d. Bank statements
   e. Tax returns
   f. Unemployment compensation verification
   g. Medical bills and/or reports
   h. Divorce decree
   i. Any other documentation to support the hardship letter

4) Contract for sale

5) Two market appraisals from local agents

6) Short sale transaction worksheet (see below)

7) List of required repairs

8) Contractor estimates

9) Details of adjustments/arrears required to be paid up front on sale e.g. levies, rates, land tax

10) List of other properties for sale or that have sold in the area (RP Data)

11) Photos of the property, inside and out.

One of the most important items in the short sale presentation package is the short sale letter to the lender. It is a covering letter stating the insolvency of the borrower, and listing all the items that are included in the package. It comes from you, the investor/purchaser.

We want to show the lender that the buyer is no longer able to make the payments, and that a mortgagee sale is the last and only option. Market data should be included and mentioned in this letter as verification that the market value of the property has dropped. This shows the lender that they stand to lose at a mortgagee sale because they can't sell the property for what is owed on it.

Basically, as shown in the example letter below, we want to give the lender a summary of the facts and situation, and list all the supporting documents included in the package.

Your job is to document the borrower's and the property's situation to convince the lender this is the best alternative. Chances are, the lender has never been to the property, and is only looking at numbers on a screen along with hundreds of other cases. You have to make an impression.

DETERMINING THE SHORT SALE OFFER

A property can be valued in a variety of ways. You might get an appraiser to do a full appraisal, using the approved method and producing a comprehensive valuation report. However, it is rarely done this way in a short sale situation. The lender is usually relying on one or both of an automated valuation module (AVM) or a valuer's opinion. The computerised AVM takes data from comparable sales in the area to estimate value.

The valuer's opinion can be either a drive-by or a more thorough inspection of the property. A lot of drive-by valuations are not done at all and are only computerised or prepared by in-house bank staff. Obviously, with this style of valuation the lender can't be sure of the interior condition of the home, or even know if the nonvisible, rear-side of the home is not grossly damaged or missing.

REAL ESTATE RESCUES

In a short sale package delivered to the lender, we want to be sure to present a full and detailed value estimate that includes the condition of the home, and the condition that will enable it to sell in the marketplace.

You don't want to own every foreclosure property. This sounds obvious, but sometimes beginning investors try too hard to make every deal work. Most deals won't - that's just the nature of the game. In this section, we take a look at how to decide whether the deal has legs or not quickly. When you're looking at lots of properties, you can't afford to spend too much time weeding out the bad deals.

EVALUATE THE INVESTMENT POTENTIAL

A good suburb/area assessment will instantly get your mind running. Don't be afraid to take a drive around, you'll find that you can quickly evaluate any potential in a property. You will subconsciously be deciding whether to rent it or flip it. You will have a good idea of the retail price range, and what your general bottom line will be in order to make a profit.

This ability will come in time, but start out by making notes. Initially, try to make an appointment to view any home sales on the street, or drop by some open houses on a Saturday afternoon. Then work the numbers backwards. I begin with a general market price, then I subtract 37 per cent to allow for sales commissions, marketing, holding costs and other incidentals, another five per cent for a below-market sale (in case I need to reduce the price for a quick sale), and 10 to 15 per cent for repairs. Then I subtract from that my required profit margin, and I am left with a rough estimate of acquisition.

- Listing price — $500,000
- Marketing and sales commission — ($35,000)
- Quick sale incentive — ($25,000)
- Repairs and renovation — ($75,000)
- My minimum profit — ($50,000)
- Maximum acquisition — $315,000

This means that unless I can get the property for $315,000 or less, it won't make sense to pursue it. Is a 10 per cent return good enough? Sometimes yes, and sometimes no. But make sure you add in what you need to clear to make the deal worth your while. The numbers will vary depending on the suburb and property assessment, but this assessment helps weed out a lot of properties upfront.

FINDING AND INVESTING IN MORTGAGEE REPOSSESSIONS

Now that you have a solid foundation and an understanding of the pre-foreclosure market, it is time to put your business into gear, and go and make some money.

FINDING THE SELLERS

With today's technology, finding sellers has never been easier. There are numerous online chat rooms, electronic classifieds, MySpace, and Facebook-type sites where people post everything about everything. You can even locate distressed owners on YouTube. Also search for the terms, "motivated seller, reduced home for sale", or "real estate for sale". You will get multiple hits from people trying to sell for various reasons. You can also utilise people finder sites if you need to locate sellers who have moved out and haven't left any contact information. Try looking in your daily newspaper Monday to Friday where they publish Court Notices or Public Notices. There you will find the names of people who are having their homes repossessed under the Supreme Court Notices for your state. They will appear under "Civil Claims" with the heading and may even have its own list entitled "Possessions". You can also find Death Notices here as well as divorce lists and bankruptcies. It is then quite easy in this information age to conduct an owner's name search through services like RP Data (www.rpdata.com.au) or Australian Property Monitors (www.apm.com.au).

LETTING SELLERS FIND YOU

Sometimes it is easy to forget that sellers are looking for us too. Thousands of homeowners around the country are thinking right now, "I wish there was someone to take this house off my hands." So you have to ask yourself, "Am I easy to find?" They won't look long.

Even with the advent of the Internet, desperate people still go to the newspaper. Call it habit or whatever, it is still a fact. At 2am, they are looking at the classifieds because they can't sleep. You need to have an ad for them. One that simply tells them you are the one they are looking for. Ads like these work: "Investor seeks houses to buy", "Can't make your next house payment? Call me" or "Don't let the bank take your home from you, if you want to sell now, I want to buy now." Distressed owners will call.

HOW TO PROPERLY CONTACT AND INTERACT WITH HOMEOWNERS

A large part of your success will be based on your ability to read people. If you can quickly discern what to say to whom, at what time, and for how long, you will have more success than you can imagine.

People in general are terrible communicators. Those who are good communicators are much more successful in getting a deal done and in building strong relationships with sellers. When seeking out properties, you must follow common sense first, and business sense second. There are entire academic studies on the theory of "first things". This basically says people give more credibility to what's first than what is second. Your job is to beat everyone to the punch, be first in line, and then more often than not, you will be the first to eat.

Remember, you will be there to solve the problem, not present a new one. Communicate like a problem solver, not an investigator. There will be rejections, and a lot of them, but rejection is like fuel for your car, you can't get anywhere without it.

In this next section, we discuss communication, common sense, and how to better handle your emotions and manage theirs.

WHY DIRECT MAIL WORKS BEST

When a homeowner is in distress, a ringing phone becomes a sound they don't want to hear. The very thought of picking up the phone sends distressed people into panic. The lesson? Don't call!

If there is anything that is more disturbing than the constantly ringing phone (mostly from bill collectors and creditors), it is the unexpected knock on the door. Be wise; engage in communication from a distance. Distance is good. It reduces pressure and allows people to think. It's also cheaper for you, and sorts out motivated vendors from those who are in denial. Distance can also keep things more professional and keep emotions at bay that otherwise would spill out if you were standing face to face.

REAL ESTATE RESCUES

Ideally, you want a homeowner to contact you. The very act of him or her picking up the phone to call gives you the immediate advantage. This is why I like to direct mail so much, it gets the homeowner involved. Yes, you have to send out quite a few pieces, and the response may be proportionally minimal, but this is a numbers game. Direct mail responses are quality responses and give you a higher probability of doing a deal. Plus, with an Excel tracking sheet, software and computer mail merges, it's easy to send out hundreds of pieces at a time.

When you send out mail, never send anything that remotely resembles a bill. Remember, that is their problem, they can't pay their bills. If your letter looks like another bill, you have just wasted the stamp because it's going into the bin. Also, never put the word "bank", "mortgagee" or "debt" on the envelope. Think about it this way: imagine you were up all night trying to think of a way to get more money and the following morning you go to the mailbox. What would you want to see? What type of mail would prompt you to open it? Probably one that looked more personal, and a bit more sentimental, maybe with handwriting on the envelope, as opposed to corporate junk mail. Homeowners in this situation are seeking relief - emotional and financial.

You are selling relief, so package your mail accordingly. I use ordinary mail, 60 cent stamps, computer typewritten on plain copy paper printed with a colour logo, and plain envelopes. No bells and whistles, straight down the middle. Another reason I do this is you don't want to publicise their problem to anyone. If they think your piece of mail just alerted the postman to their problems, the door will be shut to you forever. Respecting peoples' privacy is good for business.

Don't be afraid to address the individual with "Dear Mr/Mrs/Ms (homeowner's name)". One thing to remember is that the general practice of credit collection is designed to degrade a person while asking them for money. This is a terrible philosophy and violates everything about human nature, but nevertheless they continue to do it. We are going to respect human nature and never call someone by his or her first name until we've established a relationship. Use the appropriate courtesy titles of Mr, Miss, or Mrs every time. Debt collectors are notorious for not using courtesy titles, so it never hurts to be respectful and it might be just what you need to start a dialogue. Finally, sign a letter personally with your name, not the name of your business.

Mailing letters in a format that escalates in tone and urgency can be a very powerful tool. You will get different responses at different stages, but the key is to send them out constantly and match the tone with the escalation of the homeowner's situation.

Homeowners respond best to letters offering to relieve negative emotions, rather than letters based on logic.

Presenting a spreadsheet of how you are going to make their financial situation better is of no help. Presenting a letter detailing how you understand what they're going through and how you can realistically reduce stress is the way to go. Be firm, serious, and stress the magnitude of what they are about to experience.

Track your letters in an Excel spreadsheet or through some other organisational software. This is a great tool because you can track what letter went to whom on which date. Once you have several potential situations at the same time, you are going to need to make sure you don't miss anything. One of the biggest mistakes well-meaning investors make is assuming they can write as well as they speak. Writing is a very different skill set. Most of the greatest speakers in history didn't write their own speeches.

Unless you are a writer with proven success from your letters, you would be better off hiring a journalism student from your local university to compose text. Again, writing effectively is a skill set all unto itself; don't discount the skills required to do it. You can get experts in their fields these days to do specialist work for you cheaply and easily online – go to www.elance.com for more information.

FIRST, TRY TO HELP
Help me, help you…In the end this helps everybody!

When a homeowner is far behind in payments, many times they can't see the forest for the trees. Emotions are blinding. Before offering to take the home off their hands, make sure they have explored all the other available options. The point is to be a resource for relief. If there is a way the homeowner can save the home and it isn't you, guess what? You still win! If they ever get in trouble again, you'll be the first one they call. Many deals are not done the first time round. Your first contact may just establish to them that you are knowledgable and willing to help. You never know where your profit will come from down the line.

You want to explore the homeowner's assets and family resources with them. Walk them through the thinking process. Make sure that every possible financial resource is tapped out. This does two things: it allows you to estimate the seriousness of the situation while showing the homeowner the same thing, how serious this is. By the time you've spoken about all options and you're the only one still standing, they have actually made your argument for you. Again, it's a win-win-win scenario.

Make sure that the owner has explored reinstating the loan, a forbearance agreement, refinancing, hardship relief and so on - everything possible to keep their home from being repossessed. You can probably tell that you must strike a nice balance between what is profitable for you, and what profits the homeowner. Think of it this way, whatever profits the homeowner through your purchase or your advice, actually profits you. You are setting yourself up as a specialist, and you will sleep better at night knowing you're doing the right thing.

At the end of the day, people in distress know other people in distress. The person whose home you help them keep becomes your free marketing representative. They will spread the word.

This is a sample script that can be used during your first communication with the homeowner. When you speak with them, have your homeowner profile worksheet (in the resources section) ready to fill out.

If they call you:

HOMEOWNER: "Hello, can I speak with (your name)?"

YOU: "This is (your name), can I help you?"

HOMEOWNER: "Yes, this is (their name), and I am calling about the letter you sent me."

YOU: "Thank you for calling (their name), I am a mortgagee repossession specialist, not a real estate agent, and I contacted you to see if I might be able to help you out."

REAL ESTATE RESCUES

If you call them back:

YOU: "Hi, this is (your name), and I appreciate you calling me regarding the letter I sent you. I know it's a rough time you're going through right now, and you're being contacted by a lot of people. Despite what they tell you, there are several options available to you. I am a specialist in this area, not a real estate agent, and I contacted you to see if I might be able to help you out.

"To start, can I ask you a few basic questions about your situation? I promise that everything will remain strictly confidential."

Ask questions

Ask key questions to weed out "undoable" deals quickly. If the situation is a lost cause, politely explain that in this situation it does not appear that you can be of any assistance. Suggest that they speak with legal counsel about the situation, and wish them well.

If the deal has possibilities, then continue as follows:

YOU: "I know you are anxious to get this problem solved, and I would like the opportunity to come and meet with you and view the property. When is the earliest you would be available? Do you have time later today, or would tomorrow be better?"

(Make the appointment!)

Now let's discuss gathering the key information on the property.

VERIFYING CRITICAL PROPERTY INFORMATION

It would be nice if everyone involved in the transaction was honest and had perfect memory recall. Unfortunately, that's just not the case in most real estate deals. This is even truer if the homeowner has lived there for many years. When large public corporations buy smaller companies, they do what is called due diligence on the company being purchased. This involves a very thorough examination of all the company's historical and business records. They send in a team of auditors to go over the books for years back. It's the only way they will move forward with the huge amounts of money at stake.

You are the corporation in this case. The purchase you're about to make is not for billions of dollars, but it is certainly enough of a chunk of money to deserve your own due diligence. Your research must be very thorough and you don't have the luxury of taking months to do it. To get on track, stay that way, and finish in a time frame that will hopefully work for the lender, you must have a plan and follow it.

If, after the initial conversation, you can see that there is potential in the deal, then we need to go hunting for facts. We start with fact gathering at its most basic level: interviewing the homeowner.

Owners want quick information based on sketchy details. As investors, we want to take our time and gather all available data in order to make a solid assessment.

Your first step, as I mentioned, is to set up a meeting with the homeowner in person. Be courteous but professional, and be sure that they understand that it might take a while, and to set aside

REAL ESTATE RESCUES

the time necessary (usually one to two hours). If their home is full of family so that there isn't a quiet place to meet, it might take a little longer, but meet them at the property.

The kitchen table is the best place to meet, negotiate, and talk. It's their comfort zone, and you will be able to get more information from them. If that's not possible due to travel or it being tenant-occupied, then pick a neutral place like a nearby restaurant. This is second choice, however, because they may end up without some documentation that's tucked in a drawer somewhere at home.

I do not schedule appointments or pursue transactions with people who are addicted to drugs or alcohol, or who have serious mental issues. If there are those warning signs, I'm out of there. Not only is it going to be an uphill fight to get negotiations done, but their agreements and actions might be deemed unenforceable later on if they lacked the mental capacity to commit to the deal at that time.

If you are a woman, use some common sense and do not meet total strangers at their property at night or in a questionable environment. Meet in a public location, or go during daylight hours.

It is human nature to forget things, and this is especially true in situations like this one. You don't know this person very well at all, and yet you are asking highly personal financial questions. It is stressful for both of you. Go in with a list of questions so that you do not have to call them back to ask something you forgot. I carry extra interview sheets with me, and pull one out to fill out with the homeowner. I have included in these materials a copy of my suggested sample interview sheet.

HOMEOWNER PROFILE WORKSHEET

HOMEOWNER INFORMATION

Homeowner name/s: _____

_____

Address: _____

_____

Home phone: _____

Work phone: _____

Mobile: _____

Marital status: ☐ Single ☐ Married ☐ Divorced

Number of children: _____ Age/s:_____

Occupation: _____

Employer: _____

Referral source: _____

Why did you call? _____

REAL ESTATE RESCUES

LOAN INFORMATION

Borrower/s names/s: _____

Lender's name: _____

Lender's address: _____

Loan balance: $_____   Interest rate: _____%

Number of months behind: _____

Loan type: ☐ Conventional ☐ Non-conforming
             ☐ Private ☐ Other

Do you have any: ☐ Second mortgages ☐ Tax liens
                  ☐ Other registered interests on title

What is your estimate of the value? _____

Source? _____

Monthly payment: $ _____

Principal: _____

Interest: _____

Home in foreclosure? _____

Court date: ___/___/___

Defence filed: _____

Why are you in default? _____

HOMEOWNER ACTION STEPS

Have you had a property repossessed before?
☐ Yes ☐ No

Is it listed for sale? ☐ Yes ☐ No

Have you ever filed for or been declared bankrupt?
☐ Yes ☐ No

Bankruptcy details: ☐ Currently in
☐ Discharged on:_____

Others you have consulted: ☐ Lender ☐ Solicitor

☐ Agent ☐ Accountant

☐ Others:

What was their advice? _____

What would you like to have happen? _____

_____

Best Resolution: ☐ Cash buy ☐ Finance
☐ Repossession ☐ Short sale
☐ Rental ☐ Other

OWNER INFORMATION

Get all of the contact information for the owner: mailing addresses, phone numbers at home, at work and their mobile phones are important. You are not sure of the timeline for the transaction, nor their plans, so if possible, get some contact

REAL ESTATE RESCUES

information for relatives and friends. If the deal takes longer than anticipated, the homeowners could end up moving out suddenly. Don't be left with a disconnected phone number as your only contact.

FINANCIAL INFORMATION

If you are helping homeowners prepare the hardship letter (see below), then the owner information will need to be quite extensive, and you will want documents to back up every bit of it. You will need to ask about:

- all credit card bills and their current payment status
- the status of their first mortgage payment, how far in arrears, contact information for the lender
- all other secured and unsecured debts, equity loans, or home improvement loans
- the current payment status of all of these loans, copies of the loan documents, and contact information for the lenders
- all delinquency letters they have received for possible loss mitigation contact information
- medical bills and their payment status, delinquent notices
- divorce decree, if it is part of their financial situation.

I want to have as clear a picture of the situation as possible, the five "W's":

- What is the status and nature of the property?
- Where is their pressure coming from?
- Why they're at this stage?

- When they had to take action?
- Who else is involved?

To do that, I use the property loan worksheet below.

PROPERTY LOAN WORKSHEET

Property address: _____

_____

Lender's name: _____

Lender's address: _____

_____

Loan Officer's name: _____

Loan Officer's phone number: _____

Loan Account Number: _____

Original loan date: ____/____/____

Loan amount: $_____

Interest rate:_____%

Loan type: ☐ Conventional ☐ Non-conforming

☐ Private ☐ Other

Assumable? ☐ Yes ☐ No

Do you have any: ☐ Second mortgages ☐ Tax liens ☐ Other caveats?

Monthly payment: $_____

REAL ESTATE RESCUES

> Principal: _____   Interest: _____
>
> Taxes: _____   Insurance:_____
>
> Date recorded:_____/_____/_____
>
> Unpaid principle balance: $ _____
>
> Total payments in arrears: $ _____
>
> Total interest, late charges and legal fees: $_____
>
> Total amount needed to cure: $ _____
>
> Court or other deadline date:____/____/____
>
> Notes: _____
>
> _____
>
> _____
>
> _____
>
> _____
>
> _____

PROPERTY INFORMATION

You will probably need to conduct RP data and other legal and title searches at this step, but first let's see what you can do to make your job easier obtaining the information from the homeowner. When you set up the interview appointment, ask them to get together every document they have that pertains to the ownership of the property. They may need to go to a safe deposit box, or solicitor's office, so give them a little bit of notice.

Ask them to make copies for you, or offer to make copies and get them the originals back (immediately). Everything they can give you will be one less document you'll have to pay to have printed at the Land Titles Office.

Prompt their memory by asking them to dig up everything they can, including:

- Original deed copy

- Plan or survey

- Insurance policies

- Their contract for sale from when they bought the property.

PROPERTY CONDITION INFORMATION
If there have been any recent repairs or structural work done, get all the paperwork you can get on them. There could be a caveat involved, but you also want to know about any past problems that could relate to the current value. Have any major defects been identified? In many cases, the homeowners may have tried to sell the property on their own or with an agent. Were there any potential buyers who went far enough to get an inspection? If so, you want a copy of the inspection report if the owner has one. You also want contact information for the potential buyer because they might be a candidate for a future purchase from you. Remember, you don't know where your profit will come from.

Major defects could be anything from large slab cracks to roof damage that will require replacement. You want any paperwork or inspections that mention these things. It might just make you change your mind about doing the deal at all, or at the very least, change what you will offer to reflect repairs you'll need to make. Information is king, respect it as such.

SECURING LOAN INFORMATION

Before you begin to contact lenders and caveat holders, get a signature from the homeowner authorising you to do so. The following letter is a sample of a borrower authorisation form I use.

(Date)
(Lender rep. name, position)
(Lender)
(Street address)
(Suburb, state, postcode)

Re: Mortgage loan number _____

Dear (name)

I hereby authorise you to release any and all information regarding my loan, including payment history and balance information to (your name, address, phone). Here is the necessary information:

Borrower name: _____

Loan number: _____

Property street address: _____

Suburb, State, Postcode: _____

Thank you for your prompt assistance and attention in this matter.

Sincerely
(Borrower signature)
(Borrower name)

For some lenders this won't be enough and they will require a power of attorney for the state the property is in (power of attorney forms differ from state to state). I don't tend to use powers of attorney unless forced to because the legal document at such an early stage makes the homeowner unnecessarily fearful and suspicious. The power of attorney is limited to enabling you to talk to the lender but even so it is much more formal than a simple letter of authorisation. If you require a power of attorney for your state go to www.smokeball.com.au and download one for free.

Contact the first mortgagee first. This is the first mortgage holder, and they will be the one who typically will be deciding whether a repossession will go forward, how fast, or whether a short sale will happen. Then contact any other parties registered on the title. Use the same procedure with each, letting them know the situation and negotiating with them as to settlement of their claims, in light of the borrower's financial situation.

Of course, negotiating with other creditors registered on the title will be a bit different, as many will be losing all or most of their investments, which are subordinate to the senior lender. The key is that you must end up with a clear picture as to how much is likely to be forgiven and what may be left to pay to liquidate the claims. I tell the creditor that the debtor is in big trouble and they may not get paid at all.

CALCULATING EQUITY

I don't know about you, but I think that this is a lot of work. You've met with the homeowner, pried into their financial privacy, done RP Data research and other legal searches, haggled with multiple lenders, and examined the home for condition and repair issues. You may even have commissioned and obtained repair estimates from contractors as well. All of this research and

REAL ESTATE RESCUES

negotiation has one purpose: to arrive at the number reflecting the equity or profit potential in the home if you continue with this deal.

Remember, you are not actually negotiating to buy their property, you're effectively negotiating for the equity.

You have also gone out and gathered comparable information on sold properties, as well as detailed listing information on properties for sale right now.

Now we are tallying the results. What is your plan for the property? For example:

- If you are planning on flipping it, what do you expect to clear after repairs and rehab?
- If you are keeping it as a rental, what is your return expected to be?
- Do you have a buyer ready, perhaps through assignment?
- What are all the acquisition costs, including satisfaction of caveats, legal costs, Stamp Duty and repairs?
- What do you think the owner and lender will expect from a purchaser?
- Will that number work for our purposes and profit goals?

It's all pluses and minuses. Add up the cost of acquisition and rehab and subtract from what we are getting in a flip, and if the number is positive enough, then going ahead may be the decision. After all, we've got a lot of time and effort involved already.

If we are not flipping, but keeping the property for rental, we will want to look at the equity we expect to have from day one at settlement, and the expected appreciation near and long-term. We've done an analysis of the rental market, and we have determined our cashflow. We have studied how tax advantages will help our return on investment as well. If these numbers look good, we can go ahead and get our rental property ready for a tenant.

One of the best tips for new investors is to remember that this is a numbers game. The numbers either work, or they don't. If they don't work, there are a lot of other deals waiting for you.

If the plan you have for the property isn't supported by the numbers at this point, cut your losses and end the process.

If there is a high risk of the lender not working with your purchase offer, cut your losses and move on. It is nice to help an upside down homeowner out of a predicament, but you are not a charity. You should move on to a profitable opportunity.

A FINAL WORD
The property market is very different from what it was five years ago. This has presented a perfect storm for Australian property entrepreneurs. For the first time ever our property market is in trouble. Massive debt means borrowers cannot pay and people are underwater on their loans. When property prices were on the rise anyone who got into trouble with their home loan could always just sell it to get out of the hot seat. This is now not an available solution which seems unthinkable but the fact is that supply of homes in distress is plentiful and borrowers and banks are stuck between a rock and a hard place – enter the entrepreneurs!

Entrepreneurs emerge from the population on demand, and become leaders because they perceive opportunities available and are well-positioned to take advantage of them. Entrepreneurs

REAL ESTATE RESCUES

are among the few to recognise or be able to solve a problem. Entrepreneurs are innovators who are often responsible for changing business norms, embracing new processes, products or markets.

As U.S. President John F. Kennedy once famously said:

> *"The Chinese use two brush strokes to write the word 'crisis'. One brush stroke stands for danger; the other for opportunity. In a crisis, be aware of the danger – but recognize the opportunity."*

The foreclosure crisis in the Australian housing market has presented savvy entrepreneurs with a once-in-a-lifetime opportunity. Homeowners and banks are hurting. You can be the only port in the storm for both parties and profit handsomely for your efforts – you just need to know how the system works and then fill the gaping need in the market.

Chapter 4
THE MAGIC OF eBAY

"The higher the hurdle, the easier it is to get under it."

MATT AND AMANDA CLARKSON

MATT AND AMANDA CLARKSON

Matt and Amanda Clarkson are international speakers, eBay experts and best-selling authors.

They began from a "standing start" in 2006; after only six months' selling everyday items on eBay, they had built a $50,000-a-month, automated eBay business. Even better, it only required 10 hours a week to run!

Recognising that their eBay business system was easily replicable, they decided to create the world's leading eBay education company, Bidding Buzz.

Since 2007 they've been showing people from all over the world how to create and build their own successful eBay business.

Matt and Amanda's vision and purpose are to help people change their lives by utilising the power of the world's largest online department store - eBay. They have personally coached thousands in how to become time and cash-rich.

THE MAGIC OF eBAY

ZERO TO MILLIONAIRES IN 24 MONTHS!

What if you could start your own eBay business from scratch today (even if you have no idea what you're doing *yet*), have it up and running within hours and even be making your first profits within one day?

Sound too good to be true? Well, this is *exactly* what happened to us when we began our home-based eBay business back in February 2006 from the spare room of our apartment. We had absolutely no idea what we were doing (we'd never even been on the eBay website before) but what we did have was the burning desire in our stomach for a better life than we currently had.

We were prepared to do and learn anything to change our situation at the time and, in fact, we were running out of time fast. We were feeling stressed and uncertain about our financial future and knew that it was now or never. I was 40 years young and Matt was 34.

We'd had enough of the daily struggle and knew there was more to life than worrying about money and making sure we were going to be financially secure in our latter years. And so we began our journey of trying to find a "wealth vehicle" that would put an end to life on the rat wheel we despised.

You're now about to discover how two ordinary Aussies (a carpenter and a personal trainer) went from broke to eBay millionaires in just 24 months and why we believe absolutely *anyone* who implements the required steps, with any background whatsoever, who has a burning desire for a better, more enjoyable life, can do the same.

Let's begin the journey together…

IMAGINE IF…

We started our eBay business in February 2006 from absolute scratch and within eight months we were selling a minimum of $50,000 per month. Our various businesses now take just less than 10 hours each a week to run because we've automated 90 per cent of them. These days we still have our eBay business (we sell everyday physical items) but we spend most of our time on stage and travelling the world speaking about eBay, presenting seminars to help people like you become cash and time-rich with eBay, and demonstrating how to create multiple streams of income with eBay.

One important aspect of our eBay business is the fun we've had and continue to have, especially in the presentation of our seminars. You see, when you're having fun and loving every moment of what you do, the line between work and play becomes blurred and this is the real secret to long-lasting happiness and fulfilment.

In this chapter you're about to discover how you can start an eBay business from scratch today and start profiting almost instantly - even if you've never sold a thing on eBay before. Basically this chapter is all about helping you discover a whole range of possibilities that are out there with eBay, as we take you through the outline of a proven and very successful process that we've gone through ourselves to get to where we are today with our eBay business.

THE MAGIC OF eBAY

You'll see how you could exponentially increase your income quickly and easily using advanced tips, proven strategies and jealously guarded secrets that could turn you into the next eBay millionaire.

Did you know that currently around 1.3 million people worldwide now earn their primary or secondary living selling all sorts of things to people all over the world on eBay?

Not only that, more than 300 million eBay members spend a staggering $141 million every single day on the site! This equates to US $1 billion being spent on eBay every week of the year. Imagine sharing in even just a small slice of that pie!

ALL THE GEAR AND NO IDEA

When we first met, we were virtually dead broke. Absolutely broke. I had less than nothing because I had over $5,000 in credit card debt. Amanda also had nothing and was driving around in her tired, rusty 1980-something mobile pie van, which was called the "Pie Princess". The "Pie Princess" (as her customers fondly called her in the early days) delivered home-cooked food and goodies to factory workers and construction sites all around the city twice a day.

Let's just say that the actual food van wasn't that flash (it was well and truly on its last legs) but it was always spotlessly clean and the food was always fresh and delicious. Amanda was always racing against the clock (the workers also being on strict break times) so there was never time for stuffing around, as she'd politely put it! There was money to be made and little time to do it, as the competition in her area was getting tough.

The food business was a hard slog with long working hours six days a week. After three years of getting up at 4am, cooking till 7.30am, then driving to 22 different scheduled food stops five days a week, Amanda had hit the wall and basically just couldn't face another day of cooking rissoles, pies, casseroles, and the other 30 different dishes she had on offer anymore. By the time three years had passed, she was so stuffed and angry at where she was in life, that her regulars had started calling her the "Pie Witch" instead of the "Pie Princess". She knew she had to get out…and fast. Things were looking bleak. She was dog tired, feeling older, still almost broke and felt clueless at the ripe old age of 31.

I spent many years on the tools, wondering exactly what it was I really wanted to do with my life. I finished my apprenticeship as a carpenter and I just knew that I really didn't want to keep working in that trade. I wanted to do more, but I had a lot of family and friends saying, "You've put so much into it. You're a builder now. Don't let it go. Don't waste what you've already done."

So I stuck with it for another 11 years after my apprenticeship finished, even though I didn't enjoy what I was doing. The truth was, at the time I hated it even though it's made me a much more practical and hands-on person today. I was listening to other well-meaning friends and family who really weren't giving the right advice for me.

So, when Amanda and I got together, we had no clue about making money. Amanda is six years older than me but at that stage she was no closer to understanding how to make money and create assets for the long term either. But ultimately it was fine, because for us we began the process together with nothing. We were starting our journey at our "financial ground zero" but were so ready for the changes we knew were ahead for us. After about a year or so into the relationship and still trying to figure it all out, we read Robert Kiyosaki's book, *Rich Dad, Poor Dad*.

THE MAGIC OF eBAY

When we first read that book, it was like "Where has this whole understanding of the financial world been all our lives?"

We didn't have any clue about making money; our parents hadn't taught us anything about making money, so we had to discover it for ourselves. We felt as though we had discovered gold at the time and secretly felt excited beyond belief that ordinary people like us could actually create wealth by following someone else's step-by-step success steps. Finally we had a feeling our lives were going to take a dramatic change for the better.

As we read this book our minds were being opened to ideas for making money we never thought possible or knew existed. We thought, "Gee, maybe one day we could start a company or something?"

MATT HAS A BRAIN WAVE

I spent many years working on luxury homes in exclusive up-market estates so I was constantly around wealthy people and seeing how they lived. One day I was working on a jobsite at an exclusive waterfront estate, a massive multi-million dollar mansion on the Gold Coast.

That was the day I had what I call my "defining" moment when I knew everything had to change because what I was doing wasn't taking me closer to my goals and dreams of wealth and success. I want to describe it to you in detail so you can get a perspective of how I felt at that time.

I was eating lunch and sitting on my customary seat I had made out of the concrete building blocks used to build the house. We would make a lunch spot out of whatever we had at hand, usually a few bricks on top of each other or off-cuts of timber laid across more sticks or bricks. We'd try to get out of the sun but often there was no roof on as yet, so we were constantly in the elements getting sunburnt or windblown.

I'd cover myself in sunscreen, although I was constantly getting sun spots burnt off, and because I was always cutting and drilling timber I'd always be covered in sawdust. This would then get stuck in the sunscreen, which created a sticky thick layer of gunk on my arms, neck and face. I'd think to myself, "How the hell did I end up here?" With every passing day on those building sites I grew more and more resentful with my lot in life. I was cutting wood all day but daydreaming of a better life and knew I couldn't stomach this for much longer.

This particular day, while sitting there eating my dusty jam and peanut butter sandwiches, this massive boat came into sight and stopped at the pontoon in front of the house we were working on. I didn't know much about super yachts but this boat was longer than the land we were building the house on. The boat owner was the person we were building the mansion for and he and his family were living on the boat for the entire time we'd take to build his house.

I was constantly around these wealthy people and observing them closely and I always had an abiding curiosity about what they did and how they made their money. Not really knowing anything about creating wealth, I always thought to myself, "Somehow these people are making vast amounts of money and if they can do it, then surely I can too?"

I just didn't know how – not yet!

Enough was enough and I asked this guy how he'd made his money. Usually in that type of situation I'd just chat with the owners and be as helpful as I could, bearing in mind I was just

THE MAGIC OF eBAY

the carpenter doing the timberwork, I wasn't the head contractor or builder.

So I struck up a conversation with the owner and learnt he was originally from Canada but had moved out to Australia to retire. I gathered he was still only in his 40s. I found the nerve to ask him how he had made his fortune and he told me that he had made it by creating software that was used and sold over the Internet.

I had no clue what he was talking about at the time as I had barely even used a computer. "Wow, the Internet" I thought, "this is something new, with so much buzz in the news about it, surely there has got to be something there for me too?"

I need to clarify at this point that being a tradesman is a great way to create a living and I know many successful people who can provide for themselves and their families working on the tools. There is nothing wrong with working with your hands, I just knew that it ultimately wasn't for me and that there had to be an easier, more profitable way for me to get ahead. There were only so many hours in the day, which meant there were only so many hours I could charge for working hands on.

I had a dream at the time of making $2,000 a week in passive income. I didn't know how. I didn't know what I'd do with the money. I just knew that I wanted to wake up and have money coming in even if I chose not to work that day. That was my goal.

After talking with the man with the huge boat and massive house under construction, I decided maybe the Internet was the place to look. That's when I went home to Amanda and said, "I've got to do something different. I don't know what or how yet but things have to change."

At that stage I was what some people call a "gunna" - I'm "gunna" do this, I'm "gunna" to do that. But up until then I hadn't done anything to change my life. Thankfully Amanda was reasonably patient with my "gunna" attitude and supportive in her own way.

When I came home that day I told Amanda what I wanted to do about making money on the Internet and she finally cracked it and said: "You're always 'gunna' do this and 'gunna' do that. For God's sake just do something or stop your bloody whinging! I'm sick of you going on with all your ideas and doing nothing about it!"

Exactly how I expected her to respond. No surprises there.

I realised that I needed to do something serious. I needed to make a change in myself so that I could truly reach the potential I saw for my life. And that's when I made the serious decision to sell all of my tools. As a carpenter I needed them to work with every day to make my living. I thought to myself, "I can't come back to these tools; if I don't do something drastic, I'm going to be here in another 20 years' time."

We had a mortgage to pay, bills mounting up every week like everyone else, and I had a wife who loved to buy shoes. Luckily, Amanda was as keen as I was for a better life so she trusted my gut feeling and went along with what I did next.

I sold all my tools plus another investment property we had a bit of equity in to fund this new adventure. We were that serious.

IF IT'S TO BE, IT'S UP TO ME
Because we were coming from such a low base of knowledge, (zero actually), we knew that we had to begin the journey of educating ourselves. At the time I also had a friend who was

THE MAGIC OF eBAY

quickly becoming an Internet expert on how to use it to make money. It really is amazing how things start "to happen" once you "put it out there" as they say.

I called this friend and asked him what I should do if I wanted to get into the Internet. He told me I needed to begin educating myself on how to do it and also told me about a number of seminars I should attend in the United States, as they were well ahead of us here in Australia. So we flew to Nashville in America and went to an Internet marketing seminar that had a whole line-up of speakers with different skills and experiences. Each of the seminar speakers would have an hour-and-a-half to explain the concept of their success on the Internet and at the end of their time on stage they would give you the opportunity to purchase their individual system.

All this was so amazing and new to us. We just had no clue people would be able to find such a vast array of professionals in a field who could show you how to learn from them and replicate what they had been able to do. That was the beginning of our journey of educating ourselves so we could fast-track our results and learn from people who had already blazed the trail.

We had a lot of mixed results when we first started selling on the Internet and we certainly weren't breaking any records. We were just sort of figuring it out as we went along. And luckily I had a supportive person who was there with me all along the journey.

We were prepared to sell our only asset to educate ourselves. So, you have to ask yourself - and you might want to write your answer down - what are you prepared to do to change your current situation? Because, if you don't do something different, nothing is going to happen and you'll wake up in years to come no better off than you are now.

We were running out of time fast and spending money was far less painful than time wasted trying to work it out for ourselves. We'd already lost enough of that.

We sold a block of five units to get the money to educate ourselves because we didn't learn this stuff at school. No one else is going to teach you or educate you. It's up to you to find your right mentors and follow in their proven steps because no one cares about your outcome like you do.

We have a saying, and you might want to write this down: "Never ask the opinion of someone who does *not* have the result you want, because they are just not qualified."

It's the biggest lesson we've ever received through the benefit of having mentors. It will mean gaining new friends and losing many old ones along the way so be prepared. Your friends and family don't want you to change - it makes them feel uncomfortable so they'll often try and talk you into sticking to "what you know best". What, best for them or best for you?

When it comes to mentoring advice, your relatives and well-meaning friends are probably clueless unless they have outstanding success in the area you're interested in. If your parents, your brothers, sisters or your best friends haven't got what you want, don't ask for their advice on what you want to do. In fact, don't even mention it because if we'd listened to those who "reckoned" they knew better and that making money on the Internet was a scam or impossible, we'd still be bloody broke!

Back to finding the answer...

As I was saying, we were having mixed results making money the traditional way as Internet marketers. That's where you

THE MAGIC OF eBAY

build a website, drive traffic (potential customers) to it, begin the process of marketing to gain their confidence and finally sell something to them, either a physical product or information.

While I understood and enjoyed this process, Amanda really struggled with the whole concept and just didn't enjoy it – mainly because she needed certainty when it came to knowing how much money was coming into our account on a weekly basis. She liked to plan and know that a certain amount was coming in, week in and week out. With Internet marketing it's kind of hard to know how much money you'll make because it depends on the sales you make through your own marketing abilities.

No matter how hard she tried, she just didn't get it, nor did she like it. She was once again feeling frustrated and worried about time ticking by, but I wasn't about to give up. Not by a long shot.

And then the answer finally appeared from out of the blue…

Quite by accident one day in February 2006 we discovered eBay and it was the turning point in our lives. The lights in Amanda's head went on instantly when she was on the eBay website and could see from the information available that anyone who put their heart and mind into this business could quite literally make a fortune.

It was simple to understand, very little risk, the customers were there, and best of all, they were spending a massive one billion dollars a week!

You see, with eBay, you don't have to get your own traffic (customers) to the website like you do with traditional Internet marketing. This is all taken care of and all you need to do is sell things that people want. It's simple really – the whole eBay website is run on the "supply versus demand" philosophy. In other words, sell things people want to buy and you're in business!

This made perfect sense to both of us (Amanda was on a high because she'd finally found the missing link) and we wasted no time in getting the best mentors in the world to fast-track the process and get us into the top five per cent of sellers who really know how to make the money. And fast.

During those first few months of being mentored and learning the ropes, we were making around $800 a week net profit, selling everything around the house that wasn't nailed down. Mainly books, DVDs, CDs and videos as well as household bits and pieces. I think the turning point for us was the fact that we were making money within 48 hours of putting up our first auction on eBay and although we made many mistakes we still made a profit of $133.50. Not much I know, but for Amanda it was proof that absolutely anyone could do this; we got instant financial gratification which in turn gave us even more hope and determination and with the right mentoring we knew we could quickly and easily get out of the rat race we were in.

There was no stopping us. We were at it daily and the money just kept rolling in. We were having a ball and we'd never been as happy. Amanda got to know everyone at the post office, which was all she really had to do each day. Could you handle that? ;-) We even took a trip to America and we brought along some books and DVDs we were selling on eBay so we didn't have to shut the business down. We were selling in America anyway so we simply posted them out as we sold them. In fact, most of our sales happened while we were sitting on the plane high in the sky! Gotta love that!

THE MAGIC OF eBAY

We got serious, found new, untapped markets and worked diligently on building and growing it into a very lucrative business. Within eight months from a standing start we were making more money than we *ever* had before. We'd automated our daily tasks to the point where it was now taking less than 10 hours a week to run. The automation process was incredible to us because never before had we had so much spare time on our hands.

We were no longer selling books and things but had found our "niche" market after doing our research and to this day we still sell the same physical things after three years. The beauty of our business is that we've created a saleable asset because it no longer requires us to do any daily tasks.

WHEN YOUR DREAMS BECOME YOUR REALITY

"All I (Matt) want is an easy business that makes us around $2,000 profit every week on the Internet, doing a few hours work but mostly all automated. Just something boring and uncomplicated where I don't have to think too much but something that's fun too." This was in December 2005.

It was now August 2006…

Here's how our days would pan out. We'd get up around 6am (Amanda was still the task master) and we'd train for an hour each morning. We lived in a lovely apartment overlooking the blue Pacific Ocean on the Gold Coast. It was Amanda's dream view. She lived for her running. She'd run barefoot on the soft sand for about 10km, go for an ocean swim and lift weights. I'd go to the gym or go surfing and do my thing too. I loved my "cave time" each morning and I always looked forward to getting home afterwards to see how much money we'd made the night before. Amanda wouldn't allow business to come before our morning training sessions. Good motto I suppose but checking the bank account was the first thing I wanted to do each morning, let me tell you!

We'd then sit down and chat over a long breakfast about things we wanted to do, places we wanted to see and ways in which we wanted to expand our business. The best part of my day was opening my laptop to take a look in my PayPal account. This is our main eBay banking system (PayPal is an eBay-owned company) and I love seeing the money magically appear overnight as it does seven days a week!

Then, around 9.30am we would spend no more than two hours getting the parcels ready to post for the items we had sold on eBay the night before. By 11.30am we were finished and we only had to wait for the courier to collect the packages. Amanda would ask what she could do next (she was like a jumping jelly bean for God's sake!). "Nothing to do" was my usual reply.

She'd ask me the same question over and over but the thing was, I'd automated our eBay business to the point where there just wasn't that much to do. We were so excited we had to pinch ourselves because we couldn't believe this could be really happening for us.

We'd fill our days planning our life and what we wanted it to look like and because we had the time to "think" we actually achieved all the goals we set out for during that first year. Our relationship was strong and we loved spending our days together. We were relaxed and happy because we had the "recipe"'for making as many automated income streams as we felt like. There was nothing in the world that could match that feeling for us at the time.

THE MAGIC OF eBAY

Making money on eBay was our dream business and the confidence and fulfilment it gave us is hard to describe. Finally we could buy anything we wanted and do what we wanted with whom we wanted. That "knowing" alone has been worth every second of what we'd had to do to get to that point.

After about a year of enjoying our newfound freedom, Amanda became restless because she had too much time on her hands and missed the people interaction she'd experienced with her personal training business. Apparently hanging out with me, and our Burmese cat Burnsy wasn't exciting enough for her 22 hours of the day!

As you know, I got what I had wished for but, in truth, I also needed a new challenge. We realised we both wanted to create something even bigger where it involved other people and felt that we hadn't yet reached our full potential as entrepreneurs. Far from it.

We epitomised the typical 10 years of hard work it took to become an overnight success. We realised through setting up our own automated eBay business, a winning system that virtually anyone who chose to, could copy and apply our winning principles and formulas, and also create the foundation of a fantastic lifestyle with unlimited income streams.

It was time to step up, step out and make a difference to peoples' lives like we'd never done before.

This is when we turned our proven step-by-step system into a home-study course called "eBay Magic".

Getting this life-changing information out to people like you was now our newfound mission or bigger purpose and one that would truly see Amanda and I step "into ourselves" and finally find where we fitted in the whole grand scheme of things.

Creating and writing our eBay Magic home study course took us 10 months of working up to 100 hours a week between us. This was the biggest project we'd ever taken on, an enormous job neither of us was really prepared for but we were on a new mission and nothing was going to hold us back. More and more people wanted the eBay lifestyle too and so it was a natural progression for us to want to share what we did and how we did it with others like you.

It had never occurred to us to keep our secrets to ourselves. It's not our nature and after having spent in excess of $250,000 on mentors and education since we left school, we knew that to "give back" was even more rewarding than receiving. What goes around comes around. We are blessed with an abundance mindset. There is more than enough for us all.

Amanda was now in her element sharing, teaching and motivating others and loving every second of it. So many of our eBay Magic customers were finding financial success too so we knew we'd made the right decision. When you receive emails from people all over the world sharing how you've had a positive impact on their lives and how our eBay course has completely changed their financial destiny for the better, you feel all the work you've put in is so worth it.

I too had finally found my path and I now spend a lot of my time thinking of ways to expand our eBay education company and help as many people become cash and time-rich with eBay as we can.

But enough about our story…

THE MAGIC OF eBAY

Back to you. Are you ready, willing and able to start living life on your terms today?

If setting up your own automated cash and time-rich eBay business is right for you (we'll be getting to the nuts and bolts about that soon) then it's still going to mean rolling up your sleeves and working in your business initially and it's still going to mean putting in the time up front and it's still going to require self-management. But all these things are achievable because we've been able to do it and so have hundreds of our customers. Now it's your turn.

The changes we had to make were vast and it will be the same for you. The biggest change we had when we started this journey from broke to where we are today was leaving the negative people behind. Do you know what we mean by that?

It's hard and it's challenging, but the truth is you end up becoming just like those you hang out with the majority of the time. We're not saying leave your friends and family behind; we're saying just think about who your 10 closest friends are or the 10 people you spend most of your time with - we guarantee that your income will be within five to 10 per cent of their income.

Think that's kind of scary? Birds of a feather…It was true for us so we made a point of getting around those people who made our income look pathetic! And it worked.

Our conversations became different and so will yours. We made new friends, and so will you; we saw some old friends less and we began to think differently, so will you. And most importantly, our actions were totally different to what everyone else was doing. And yours will be too.

We began to grow and evolve into what it took to go from broke to multi-millionaires. And so will you. It was never going to happen any other way.

When we started our eBay journey, we were often laughed at by well-meaning friends. Some of you have heard the story where we went to a barbeque and some old friends laughed while asking, "How's your little eBay business going these days?"

They stopped laughing when we casually told them we were turning over around $50,000 a month at the time. "You're doing what? Can you tell us what you sell so we can do the same? Can you give us your program for free?" You know, all the usual lines.

Amanda just laughed and said "No, don't worry, you wouldn't want to know. It's not for you!"

They're not laughing anymore though. The truth is that often when people laugh at you when they see you want to make a change they're embarrassed and don't want you to leave them behind. It's painful for them to see that you want something better for yourself while they're happy to live in denial and ultimately pain.

Interestingly enough, those who laughed at us the most never asked us how we did it or if they could invest in some education or ask, "What did you learn to get the results you have today?"

We went through a lot of changes to get where we are today. Most of you would agree that someone who progressed from a hands-on carpenter to an onstage seminar presenter, teaching sophisticated eBay strategies all around the world, had to make some changes. Old friends or family were asking, "What are

THE MAGIC OF eBAY

you doing? Don't you want to be one of us anymore?" Those sorts of things.

The good news is you can become whomever you want without changing who you are. The most important thing you'll need to do when you've finished reading this book is to be confident, persistent and take massive action. And of course, be optimistic because you will get *exactly* what you expect.

If you think that this will work for you then you're absolutely right and if you think it won't or can't then you're absolutely right again! It's how we think and feel about things that will cause the outcome whether good or otherwise. Understand that your ultimate goal may not happen for you instantly and that's okay - it's not a race - it's a matter of just being persistent and following through with the action steps that others have proven to work.

Become true to yourself and act on what you say you're going to do for yourself and for your family.

We learned a great lesson while on this journey we want to share with you: if you're on your journey to a better life, whatever that is for you, and you're with someone who isn't, then you must align your values (the things that are most important to you and high on your agenda) so that you can strive for the same outcome. Otherwise it won't be easy.

Your values at this point in life right now might be wanting to make money and wanting to become more secure. If your business or life partner has different values to you then you must find out what they are and align them before you begin. We know for certain that if you're on the same path with the same goal in mind, the road will much easier, smoother and far more enjoyable.

Also, practice making quick and decisive decisions, whether they are right or wrong. It doesn't matter. You'll have a result. The people in this world who go on to create wealth and lifestyles to die for, have the ability to make fast decisions. They are the action takers. They are *not* procrastinators. The truth is, if you want something different, you will have to do things you've never done before. Are you prepared for this?

WHY THERE HAS NEVER BEEN A BETTER TIME TO MAKE UNLIMITED INCOME WITH eBAY

In all our years of being in business, never have we seen an opportunity for making unlimited income streams like we have with eBay. With over 50,000 categories to choose from and a never-ending supply of buyers, all you need to do is discover all those hot untapped markets and give the buyers what they want.

Every day more than 70,000 new members flock to eBay looking to buy and sell all sorts of interesting things. More and more people are now turning to the Internet looking for bargains and it's a fact that 75 per cent of eBay buyers earn in excess of $50,000 a year and spend an average of two hours on eBay each time they visit.

There is, of course, a bit behind the scenes but in a nutshell, if you remember this one principle you're on your way to eBay riches if you follow all the necessary success steps. Oh yes, and here's a very important tip…

Never assume what someone will or will not buy on eBay. You have no idea what they are thinking when placing bids or buying up so keep your assumptions to yourself!

Live by this golden rule, follow all the steps in the recipe and you will make money on eBay - simple as that.

THE MAGIC OF eBAY

Funnily enough, in many cases eBay shoppers buy because they are bored, want to spend money and just love the whole shopping experience. Hard to believe - but true.

You've probably heard of some crazy eBay stories yourself where people pay astronomical amounts of money for weird or sometimes seemingly worthless items?

We have some friends in the US who divorced. As the ex-husband was preparing the house for sale, to his utter disbelief in one of the cupboards he opened, he found 130 unopened eBay packages the ex-wife had bought.

She was addicted to shopping on eBay and just loved the "rush" of winning the auction. Amanda offered to take the parcels off his hands and resell them on eBay but I warned her not to go there!

Around 90 per cent of eBay sellers are what we call "hobbyists" and often aren't interested or simply have no idea how to create a highly profitable business. They sell things on eBay as an extra stream of income and more often than not they put things up to sell and simply "hope for the best".

Not a smart way to run a business if you want it to be a long-term income stream though. Because they're uneducated when it comes to knowing how to maximise profits on eBay and simply just copy everyone else, they end up making minimal profits and often blame eBay's fees and charges for their failures. Here's where you can get the edge and cash in on other people's laziness and ignorance!

Copying what "the masses" do on eBay is a recipe for financial disaster let alone the time you'll waste. There is no point in starting *any* business unless you know exactly how to maximise all your efforts. Why would you bother? People are often extremely surprised at how much we invest into our "business education", however, once they understand how much financial return we get, they're in awe.

Remember this: spending money on education is an INVESTMENT and not a cost. If your education is for business purposes it should be tax deductible and even if you need to go into debt for it, as long as you know you can get a great return, then we call that Good Debt.

Bad debt is when you spend money on things that lose value, things like cars, TVs and impulse items that give you short-term gratification. Education *can and will* set you free if you put what you learn into action! It's a fact and one that Matt and I are so very passionate about because we do exactly as we preach. It's no mistake that we are where we're at today; it's simply our return on investment and you can experience this too.

One of the early lessons we learnt when selling on eBay was to make absolutely sure the "Listing Title" of the items we were selling was spelt correctly. Even the slightest spelling mistake might be enough to stop bidders finding your item for sale. Another interesting snippet of information is the majority of bids on eBay are placed between 9am and 5pm – normal working hours for most people. Little wonder many bosses won't allow their workers to log onto the eBay website!

eBay has 33 websites you can sell your products to the world from while working in the comfort of your own home and they have made it possible for literally anyone to make money online, *virtually instantly* with unstoppable traffic and hungry buyers – and best of all, you can start your own eBay business for absolutely minimal cost.

THE MAGIC OF eBAY

There are *thousands* of everyday Aussies and people all over the world now making multiple streams of income through this amazing platform called eBay, and with thousands of new members joining daily, there is a never-ending supply of buyers waiting to be served by you!

Creating your own eBay business that is highly profitable ultimately can give you the lifestyle you've wanted for so long if you do it right, giving you and your family peace of mind knowing you no longer have to rely on someone else for money.

FIVE WAYS TO START MAKING MAXIMUM PROFITS WITH MINIMUM COST

Our eBay Magic home study course shows you at least 10 different ways to create cashflow from eBay. This section outlines five no-cost or low-cost strategies you can start with immediately.

I (Amanda) am an expert at finding "hot, untapped" markets on eBay and could spend a whole day sharing this stuff with you because no matter what you want to achieve here, there is a way that will suit you, your time frame and your budget! And because I can't go over all the 10 ways with you today, you can always find out more if you'd like to see us speak at the next eBay Magic workshop coming up soon.

Now, what to sell in the early days?

When you're first getting started with your eBay business, the best way to go about it is to choose something to sell that is:

- of minimal value
- an unwanted item (an unwanted gift or something!)
- easy to pack and post

- not fragile
- in good, clean condition.

Here are a few ideas for you if you've come up blank!

- CDs and DVDs in good condition
- Fiction and non-fiction books in good condition
- Old comics
- Toys and hobbies
- Crockery
- Sporting goods
- Consumer electronics
- Dolls and bears
- Name brand clothing (must be dry-cleaned)
- Motivation books, tapes, videos and DVDs
- Handbags
- Leather goods
- Old records.

The reason it's important to start out by selling off your unwanted goods is so that you can grow your eBay feedback quickly to gain credibility as a seller.

You don't want to be "cutting your teeth" selling items of high value as you may lose money and in most cases you won't get as much for your item if you're a brand new seller as you would a "seasoned" seller.

THE MAGIC OF eBAY

There are reasons why you must grow your eBay business step-by-step. It's just like following a recipe - all the ingredients must be in place for the best results.

And of course, there are some things that you CANNOT sell on eBay. It's a very good idea to know about these things before you go off happily listing everything in sight! Check out the eBay Listing Policies in the help section and know the rules before you get started!

All the examples above are great ideas for you to start selling right now. This is exactly how we started our eBay business – selling off everything in the house that wasn't nailed down! We started selling books, DVDs, tapes, videos, CDs, wallets, shoes, handbags etc. In the early stages of growing our eBay business, we were making a very nice income every week just from selling things we didn't want, use or need anymore.

I'm still amazed at some of the prices we got for these items. Never assume that no one will buy what you have on offer. You do not know what other people think and feel about certain products so never try to pick the market. Let the market tell you what it wants!

eBAY MAGIC EXAMPLE ONE:
eBAY HOBBYIST

Here's where a lot of sellers start out before they work out which selling method will work best for them. A hobbyist is someone who initially sells on eBay for fun and wants to create an extra income stream on the side. It's perfect for those who have a job or business and need extra cash or for those who need more money but don't want to get another part-time job.

You can find a never-ending supply of stuff to sell from opportunity shops, bric-a-brac stores, shopping outlets, flea markets, friends and family, garage sales - and the list goes on and on.

There are no major downsides to this business at all except that it's hard to automate because you're selling a lot of "one off" items. This means you need to take photos and write up a new description for each item you intend on selling.

Having said this, I know a young lady who makes up to $1,000 a week selling items she gets from Salvation Army stores.

eBAY MAGIC EXAMPLE TWO:
DROP SHIPPING

This is a great way to start out with your eBay business if you're on a tight budget, or want to make money working on your laptop from anywhere in the world. Many people start off with a drop shipping business while "getting their feet wet" learning the ropes then move onto bigger and better things.

Drop shipping means you deal directly with wholesalers who take care of the shipping process for you. Many sellers don't like to handle stock so this is a great way to make money without doing so.

In a nutshell, you sell the items the drop shippers supply and use all their photos. They hold all the stock ready for when you sell it.

You then sell the products, collect the money from your buyer and only then do you pay the drop shipper. The difference between what you sell your product for and what you pay the

THE MAGIC OF eBAY

drop shipper is your profit. Once you pay the drop shipper, they then send the item directly to your customer and you've not handled anything except the money.

This whole process takes place *before* you outlay a cent of your own money!

There are a couple of downsides to drop shipping in our opinion. Firstly, you're relying on the wholesaler to get the parcels out to your customers, which means you don't have total control over your business and, of course, eBay is built on the "feedback" system. Also, many people are using the same drop shippers, selling the same goods. You must be careful not to sell items only to find out the drop shipper has run out of stock. Your customers won't be happy and it's your responsibility to keep them happy.

You must make sure you're dealing with "legitimate" wholesalers and there are ways to determine this quite easily.

Lastly, because the drop shipper is incurring most of the costs like warehousing, packing etc, the profit margins are smaller. It's normal to collect anywhere between five to 25 per cent or a little more depending on what types of products you're selling.

eBAY MAGIC EXAMPLE THREE:
RUN A CONSIGNMENT BUSINESS AND SELL OTHER PEOPLE'S GOODS

This is one of my favourite ways for beginners to make money on eBay. Consignment means you sell other people's stuff for a percentage of the profits. The profit is determined between you and the person who owns the goods, again, depending on what you're selling. Some sellers take up to 50 per cent after eBay costs but again, you'll just agree on what's fair at the time.

In our eBay Magic home study course, we have gone into detail about this method of selling and exactly how to go about getting a never-ending supply of products to sell. We've even supplied different ads you can copy and agreements you can use if this is for you. We even tell you how to approach the storeowners and what to say.

Once people get to know that you're an eBay magician, they will come to you in hordes asking if you will sell their stuff. It happens to us constantly and we always say no because we just can't do it all!

eBAY MAGIC EXAMPLE FOUR:
eBAY ARBITRAGE. BUY LOW, SELL HIGH. SOURCE ALL YOUR STOCK FROM EBAY AND OTHER AUCTION SITES

Arbitrage is another great method of finding stock to sell on your eBay site. There are countless eBay traders all over the world buying from eBay sellers who have listed incorrectly or listed at the wrong time. They purchase on eBay and then manage to resell at a profit.

We know of many people making part-time and full-time income streams doing this. In fact, one of our staff members loves this method of selling and makes a lot of money doing it. You can buy all different types of items from *clueless* eBay sellers (you'll soon get to know them in no time) and other auction sites or you can concentrate on a "niche" market and go for that.

THE MAGIC OF eBAY

eBAY MAGIC EXAMPLE FIVE:
SELL YOUR OWN PRODUCTS

We know of many eBay sellers who have a talent or a hobby and have been able to turn those skills into big profits by showing other people how to do the same.

For instance we know of a lady who created a DVD on how to design and make beautiful hair bows in the USA and was selling them on eBay for $99. She was selling between one to five a day which means she was selling at least $700 a week! Her profit would have been over 80 per cent, if not more.

The beautiful thing about creating and selling your own information products is the high profit margins you can make and how simple this business is to automate.

It doesn't have to be "high tech" or anything like that. You can simply use your home video or recorder to create these products. I don't really see any downside to this type of eBay business and, in fact, if you're creative and have something that others want to know about, you can create a very lucrative business indeed.

There are at least 10 other ways I could share with you. You see, there are just so many juicy ways you can be up and running on eBay in no time at all. You've just got to know what you're doing and why you're doing it. Once you've got the step-by-step system in front of you, there's no holding back and you can now see why you can create as many cashflow streams as you desire. **You are only limited by your own thoughts and beliefs.**

Finding a never-ending supply of items to sell on eBay is the easy part. Creating something of *value* though takes time, a lot of thinking and, most importantly, the right kind of action.

Don't worry though, because we've made this part easy for you. You're about to discover our eBay Magic steps to what it takes to be super successful and profitable when it comes to making money on eBay.

BRINGING IT ALL TOGETHER
Building a long-term, profitable eBay business takes precise planning just as building a high-rise building does. It's all about building a strong foundation so that the business continues to grow and stay profitable for the long term. Remember, you are building an asset here so it's important to follow all the success steps in order for this to become your reality.

We've done all the hard work for you so all you need to do is copy exactly what we've done and you too can be on the way to making more money than you can imagine if that is what you want. Remember your outcome and *stick to the plan!*

GET YOUR HEADSPACE AND MINDSET RIGHT – YOU MUST PLAN FOR YOUR SUCCESS

- Open your mind and *expect* success. If you keep an open mind it will happen for you. You know the power of positive thinking. Stay away from negative people and do whatever it takes to make this happen. There has never been a better time than today.

- Less than one per cent of sellers on eBay are educated and take eBay seriously as a business. If you were to get real serious about your outcome, what could you achieve on eBay? Can you visualise the opportunity available here from what we've shared so far?

DISCOVER HOW TO DEVELOP YOUR "PRODUCT FINDING MINDSET" QUICKLY AND EASILY

This simple technique is the answer to the million dollar questions: "What am I going to sell on eBay and where do I get it?"

Mastering this technique will ensure you *never* run out of ideas and things to sell.

Probably one of the most frustrating and difficult tasks as an eBay seller is the ongoing and time-consuming task of sourcing a regular supply of hot selling items to sell through your eBay business. Don't despair, you're not alone, because each and every eBay seller has at one stage had the same hurdles while trying to grow their business.

In the early stages of most eBay businesses, everyday people just like you generally start out by selling items they have sitting around the home that are no longer wanted, needed or used.

This includes household items, unwanted gifts, clothing and accessories you no longer wear, old records, CDs, DVDs, books, electronics, cars, furniture, toys and so on.

What happens in a lot of cases (including our own) is that once you start selling and making money on just about everything you list on eBay, all of a sudden you find yourself "hooked". Next thing, you're stalking around the house in search of anything that isn't nailed down that you can list and sell for a profit!

But as can be expected, you soon run out of things to sell from around the house. Once you've collected and sold everything you could get your hands on from your friends and neighbours, you're left with the job of sourcing an ongoing supply of merchandise.

Well, the good news is, there are quite a few ways that you can go about finding never-ending supplies of product to sell in your eBay business. But before we get into this, there are a couple of steps you'll first need to put into place.

The first and most important step is to **develop your "Product Finding Mindset".** This simply means that if you want to be "switched on" to *what's hot* on eBay, there are a few tips and tricks you can develop that will give you a great head start.

First of all, when you're going through the process of deciding what types of products you'd like to sell on eBay, you have to put yourself into the "consumer's" mindset to find out exactly what it is that they want or need to buy. Here are the four steps you need to take to ensure you develop your product finding mindset.

1) **Open-minded ideas:** Open your eyes, ears and mind to everything. The marketplace is changing constantly. What may be hot today could be cold and old news by tomorrow! Watch out for trends and think of how you can take advantage of them. Keep a very open mind here.

   The biggest mistake you can make is to *assume* you know what the market wants and doesn't want. How do you know what's going on in consumers' minds? You *don't*. And that's the point.

2) **Let the market decide what *they* want:** Your job is to bring it to them. Knowing and living by this one simple rule can make or break your eBay business. *Assumption* is one

THE MAGIC OF eBAY

of the main reasons why so many eBay sellers and Internet marketers go broke!

From today forward, your two cents no longer counts. If you conduct your market research properly you'll never have to assume what your market wants again because you'll know exactly what they want to buy.

And remember, your thoughts become your reality so if you think you won't find things to sell on eBay on an ongoing basis, you're right. But if you believe you *can* find a never-ending supply of stuff to sell, then you can practically guarantee that you will.

It's in the early stages of setting up a long-term eBay business that you'll have to be active and be patient. The deals will come to you once you get the word out that you're the master at selling on eBay. I've not met a single person who hasn't heard of eBay or one who doesn't have an "eBay story" to tell.

During this journey be open-minded and open-hearted. You'll *never* think the same way again when it comes to business.

3) **Look around you**: When you next walk into a department store, or any store for that matter, look around the place to see if you notice any "new, hot items" that have come into the marketplace. If they've made it to the shelves in department stores, they'll probably sell on eBay!

   You'll probably agree that just about every single week, a new product of some sort is introduced to the consumer market. It's a never-ending stream of products.

If you find something in a store you'd like to sell on eBay, look on the back of the packaging, and in most cases there'll be the manufacturer's details. Get on the phone and see if you can source the product. Talk to people in the store about doing a joint venture where you could sell their overstock or end of season clearance stuff.

When you get home do a "completed listings" search and see if the products you see in stores are selling well on eBay? This is how I come up with so many ideas for products. They're all around us!

Walk around with your eyes and ears wide open. You'll begin to take notice of things you've never noticed before. I find myself constantly asking myself this question: "Would *that* sell on eBay?"

4) Sell what people want to buy – not what you want to sell them.

FIND AND RESEARCH HOT, UNTAPPED MARKETS
To be successful on eBay you need to get into the minds of your customers. What new products are people talking about? Can you sell them on eBay? To really get an edge, you need good market research.

Research is a critical part of your eBay business for long-term success. Have an abundance mindset – not a "lack of" mindset. You will get what you expect every time! There is an abundance of items suitable for sale on eBay – do your research and find them.

Research is about building the foundations of your business just as if you were building your home – it is serious stuff. Use all of your powers of observation while researching for new products

THE MAGIC OF eBAY

– you never know when or where you might come across the next opportunity. Your local newsagent has a huge range of inexpensive specialist magazines you can use to research product ideas.

Trade shows, industry magazines and even junk mail are other excellent sources for researching new products. Never second guess what the market wants to buy.

Ultimately your research should produce a product that has a backend for ongoing income. The term "backend sale" applies to making an initial sale to a customer and then developing an ongoing sales relationship. Instead of just one sale and losing contact with the customer, by capturing the details of new customers, an opportunity exists for further sales in the future.

Research is constant, continuous, fun and extremely rewarding when you find a gold nugget! Again, we've made this simple for you. We show you exactly how we find hot, untapped markets on eBay using very simple software programs. We never sit there wracking our brains for ideas! Who's got time for that?

DECIDE HOW YOU WANT TO SELL YOUR ITEMS

Auction format: When you decide to choose the auction format, you'll need to set a starting bid. This is mandatory and can be as low as one per cent or as high as you choose, but keep in mind that if you start your bidding too high, potential bidders will be turned off because they want to feel like they may be able to snap up a bargain.

By starting your bidding low, you'll definitely encourage bidders to bid on your auction and with a bit of luck, your auction may even start a bidding war. People seem to take more interest in auctions that already have bids on them.

With the auction format, you can decide on the auction duration and include a quantity if you have more than one item to sell. You can also include a **"Buy It Now"** price if you'd like to offer the bidder the option to buy the item without waiting for the auction to finish.

This is a point you might want to think about. Of course you want to be finishing your auction when most people are online looking for your type of item.

Fixed Price format: The fixed price format or the "Buy It Now" as it's commonly known, allows you to sell items for the price you want, and not have to worry that you might lose money in an auction. These listings still appear in the standard auction search results, and have listing duration options, just like a standard auction of 1,3,5,7 or 10 days.

There are many reasons why you'd choose to sell items in this way, and in fact, you could have fixed price listings along with auction-style listings and see which gives you a better result.

Ultimately, by conducting your market research you'll know which format works best for the items you're selling, and at what price point your buyers are prepared to pay for it.

THE MAGIC OF eBAY

Good 'til cancelled format: eBay is a search engine just like Google or Yahoo and they now have some pretty sophisticated guidelines of how you actually get ranked higher, depending on a few criteria.

The system is called **Best Match** and it automatically tries to show potential customers the best person to shop from, based on the keywords they use.

For example, if you use a good 'til cancelled listing which has a set fixed price, the search engine will reward you and raise you higher in the results if you:

- have good feedback and detailed ratings from customers
- sell the same item over and over successfully

- offer free shipping
- have top rated seller status.

These criteria mean that you will potentially sell more items and essentially you become more and more successful as time goes on.

Conversely, if you do not maintain good status as a seller your listings could be sent from page one to page 31 overnight. You definitely don't want this to happen as you end up not being found.

This highlights how important it is to make sure you follow all the steps and ensure you are giving the best customer service you can.

So how do you do that and how important is it?

PROVIDE OUTSTANDING CUSTOMER SERVICE
This is by far the most important area too many eBay sellers ignore! What are they thinking? Without happy customers there is *no* business. As you've seen above, if you don't deliver great service you potentially send your listings into no man's land. You'll want to create "evangelists" as well so that your business automatically grows via word-of-mouth. You have no idea just how powerful this can be until you experience it.

It's easy to get your customers raving about your business and growing your business for you by word-of-mouth referrals if you follow the system exactly. Great service happens after the sale and even more profits can be made here. Customer service is paramount on eBay. eBay is built on the "feedback" system and knowing how to make the most of this can see you become successful beyond your wildest dreams

THE MAGIC OF eBAY

Remember, eBay customers can't see you, or get a feel for what type of person you are to the degree they could if they were to chat with you personally. You don't have a retail shopfront so it's normal that new customers may have some reservations about handing over money – this is why customer service is paramount on eBay.

Our whole business is built on referrals because we provide outstanding customer service.

We have found that around 95 per cent of eBay sellers assume the transaction is complete when the sale has been made and they have banked the money; in fact, we believe this is just the beginning. If you are friendly and kind to your customers they will refer other customers to you. This is word-of-mouth advertising - the least expensive and best advertising of all for attracting people to your business.

WHY KEEPING AND MAINTAINING A 100% POSITIVE FEEDBACK SCORE IS YOUR NUMBER ONE PRIORITY

As you'll agree, running an eBay business is quite different to running a "bricks and mortar" type of business. One of the main differences is that with an online business, your buyers or customers can't see you, so they don't know exactly from whom they may be buying.

In a bricks and mortar business, the owner has a chance to create and nurture great customer relations by providing outstanding service, a good range of products, return policies, friendly staff etc.

When you experience these "good shopping experiences", you tend to go back and shop with these people, over and over again because you know without a doubt that you will enjoy the shopping experience. Every time.

Sometimes price and location does not come into it if the experience is extremely positive.

People love to shop where they'll feel welcome and appreciated. It's a fact!

The one thing shoppers *can* see by looking at your eBay business though, is your **Detailed Seller Rating**. This feedback rating has basic information about past transactions that you have completed, and what the overall experience was like for the people you dealt with.

Every eBay member has a feedback rating. For serious eBay sellers, this rating is "jealously guarded" because your feedback rating is all you have when it comes to building your credibility in this business. Every comment about the way you conduct business, good *or* bad, counts.

The feedback shown below is a snapshot of our feedback around June 2008. It has the total amount of unique feedback left as well as a number of other icons. People on eBay love seeing the icons after your Seller ID so get as many as you can.

(5350 ☆) me 📱 ✏️ Top **100** Reviewer

dback (last 12 months): 98.9%

Detailed seller ratings (last 12 months)

Criteria	Average rating	Number of ratings
Item as described	★★★★★	660
Communication	★★★★★	659
Postage time	★★★★★	649
Postage and handling charges	★★★★★	658

THE MAGIC OF eBAY

AUTOMATE YOUR eBAY BUSINESS UP TO 90%

This is by far the most exciting aspect of having an eBay business and one that we are *very* passionate about. We love talking about the automation process because it's only through automation that you can truly be free of the day-to-day tasks of running an eBay business. Because we automated nearly 90 per cent of our own eBay business we were free to be able to create our eBay Magic home study course which hundreds of people are now using successfully all over the world.

In fact, the whole automation process is one of the main reasons why people find this such an attractive business to be involved with. We've had many businesses in the past and have never been able to automate the process like we can with eBay. This then allows you to either sit back and enjoy the fruits of your labour or move into another untapped market and go again! Truly amazing!

Below are the daily processes we can automate which frees up our time to the point where our business now takes less than 10 hours a week to run. Beautiful.

- The listing process
- Customer payment reminder emails
- eBay feedback
- Invoicing and checkout
- Payments and banking
- Item sent emails
- Data collection
- Second chance offers and much more!

For many people an automated eBay business is a serious – and fun – alternative to working long hours of paid, or worse, unpaid overtime to supplement their income.

FOLLOW PROVEN SYSTEMS AND DON'T REINVENT THE WHEEL

What can we say? Both Matt and I have gone over this point and the importance of it many times throughout this chapter. I think by now you understand and can see why we so strongly recommend you do the same.

I have a saying and you can borrow it, "You can always get more money but *never* more time."

And as one of my favourite and most respected mentors says, "Pay once, cry once" (meaning the investment into business education).

I love this because as he says, you're going to pay one way or another for your education. That's in *time or money*. Which is less painful for you right now?

These words are foremost in my mind when I'm looking at *any* business opportunity and every time Matt and I discuss business, we're always asking ourselves how we can fast-track the processes by following a *proven* system someone else has created.

I don't know about you, but I'm well over wasting precious time stuffing around trying to work things out for myself when I can simply invest in my education and avoid the heartache of costly, embarrassing mistakes.

Ask yourself the same question: do you really have time to waste trying to work all this out for yourself?

THE MAGIC OF eBAY

I think I know the answer if you truly value your time.

Are you excited about setting up an eBay business and creating the exact lifestyle that you want and deserve?

Right now, write down all the things that you'd like to be spending the extra money on and how you'd like your day to pan out if you had your own way.

Go on, start to imagine and visualise *exactly* how your own highly profitable eBay business is going to look and feel once you get cracking on it.

Okay, so now you have some of our precious "eBay Magic" juice that we can share with you up to this point in time.

For you, the next step is to take a deep breath and confidently know within yourself that anyone, including YOU can have a very, very profitable eBay business up and running as soon as next week. All you have to do now is take MASSIVE action and know that many have been there before you.

There has never been a better, more exciting time than now to get started. With over 1.3 million sellers already making either a part-time or full-time income on eBay right now, you'd be mad if you didn't want a piece of the $161,000,000-a-day action!

All you've got to do is take the first step and the rest is easy!

What are you waiting for? It's time to sell something on eBay…

Chapter 5
FOREX TRADING

"Forex is the greatest business in the world – for those who learn how to trade properly."

DANIEL KERTCHER

DANIEL KERTCHER

Daniel Kertcher is founder and CEO of Trading Pursuits, one of Australia's leading financial education companies.

Since forming the company is 2001, Daniel has presented live educational presentations and multi-day courses to more than 150,000 people on various financial topics including Stocks, Options, CFDs, Futures, Bonds and Forex trading.

Along with his team of highly-skilled professional analysts, Daniel oversees the company's proprietary trading accounts. Through their online reports the company shows their clients every trade they make in the markets - before they even place the trades!

In 2010, Daniel teamed up with the largest CFD (contract for difference) provider in the world to develop a world-first trading strategy combining CFDs with Covered Call writing.

He has been a keynote speaker at many international events along with Anthony Robbins, Donald Trump, Sir Richard Branson, Robert Kyosaki, Mark Bouris, Brad Sugars, Pat Mesiti and many others.

He has authored several books, including the bestselling *Taming the Beasts: Secrets to Profit in Volatile Bull and Bear Markets*. He has also written many articles for international magazines and newspapers in Australia, Singapore and Dubai.

He also invented the world's only Stock Market Options Trading board game: Call Up Put Down.

Daniel is a fully accredited Options, Derivatives and Futures advisor.

He lives in Sydney, Australia, and when not teaching, trading or working with his clients he enjoys travelling and spending time with his family and friends.

FOREX TRADING

THE PERFECT BUSINESS FOR THE MODERN LIFESTYLE

Before we can find the perfect business for ourselves, it's important to identify and describe the various features we want our perfect business to have. Why not take a moment now and think of some of the features your perfect business must have for you.

The following list contains the features that I believe would constitute the perfect business for the modern businessperson:

1. No staff, no customers

2. Can be controlled from anywhere in the world, online, with an iPad, smartphone etc.

3. Requires very low capital start up, without limits

4. Limitless potential

5. Very high potential returns possible

6. Limited risk

7. No administration required; automatic bookkeeping

8. Extremely low overheads

9. Highly liquid; can have your cash returned at most within two business days

10. Returns are independent of market conditions; opportunities exist in recessions, booms etc.

11. Not a fad; the business must be available for decades to come

12. Can generate regular income as well as high capital gains potential

13. Extremely low transaction costs

14. Can use leverage, allowing business owner to use other people's money easily

15. Completely level playing field; no advantages to people with larger bank balances

16. Little time required to run the business; 10-60 minutes a day maximum

17. Easy to learn, easy to do

18. Excellent training and support from highly experienced professionals available.

Let's discuss these points in greater detail.

1. **No staff, no customers** - Staff are consistently one of the greatest expenses of any traditional business, in time, money and stress. Acquiring customers requires ever-changing marketing skills and deep pockets. Retaining customers requires serious attention, service and support. Imagine having a business that has the potential to generate for you the income and capital gains you desire, without having any staff, and with no customers! Is such a business even possible?

FOREX TRADING

2. **Can be controlled from anywhere in the world** - Imagine skiing in Canada, or laying on a Fijian island beach, or shopping on Fifth Avenue, New York, all the while, being able to completely control your business from your iPad or smartphone. This is no longer science fiction. This is science reality!

3. **Requires very low capital start up, without limits** - When starting a new business, it is wise to start with a small investment, say $1,000, to allow yourself the opportunity to see if it is something you enjoy and wish to continue. Many people have invested hundreds of thousands and even millions of dollars into businesses only to find out that the business doesn't perform or that they don't even enjoy working in it. It's also important that there are no limits to the business. That is, once you decide that you like the business you should be able to invest as much money into as you wish, without any limitations at all.

4. **Limitless potential** - Once you get started, there should be no limit to how much profit you can potentially make from your business.

5. **Very high potential returns possible** - It's one thing to have limitless potential, but if you only generate a few dollars per transaction as profit, then you'll either need a huge number of transactions, or a very long time! It's important therefore that our perfect business can potentially generate substantial returns on each transaction we make, and have the ability to do many transactions. This way we can really explore the true limitless potential of our business.

6. **Limited risk** - Obviously a modern business must have limited risk. Our perfect business must allow us to control our risk at all times, and provide the opportunity to offset or insure our risk in any market condition.

7. **No administration required; automatic bookkeeping -** Let's face it, everyone hates having to do administration in their business such as keeping orderly files, accounts etc. Some people may be good at it, but that doesn't mean that they like it. I'm sure they would much prefer spending their time on more enjoyable pursuits. However, it's critical that files and accounts are kept completely up to date and accurate. Therefore, our perfect business would need to automatically and electronically keep track of itself, thus allowing us to call on any file or account in an instant.

8. **Extremely low overheads -** Our perfect business must not weigh us down with expensive overheads. And seeing as we don't have any customers or staff, we won't need an office, another usual high expense for traditional businesses.

9. **Highly liquid; can have your cash returned at most within two business days -** We all know that we live in a volatile world. Market conditions can change overnight. Many businesses that work perfectly well in one type of market may prove to be totally ineffective in other types of markets. Our perfect business must allow us complete and total access to all of our money within two business days maximum. This gives us the ability to be completely flexible and nimble.

10. **Returns are independent of market conditions; opportunities exist in recessions, booms etc. -** Opportunities exist everywhere, all the time. Our perfect business must be suitable to operate in any market condition, 24 hours a day.

11. **Not a fad; the business must be available for decades to come -** There are so many business opportunities available today such as franchises, Internet marketing, network marketing etc. Many of these businesses can be very successful for a limited time, but often require

FOREX TRADING

complete re-invention once the market has changed and/or new technology has superseded it. Our perfect business needs to have a timeless quality, that is, it is not a fad and will still be operating the same way it does today, as it will be in the many years to come.

12. **Can generate regular income as well as high capital gains potential** - An ideal business would provide both a regular daily income along with substantial capital gain potential.

13. **Extremely low transaction costs** - The success of any business is dependent on the transactions that the business conducts, and the associated costs involved. Transactional costs, such as commissions, brokerage and tax can quickly erode returns. Our perfect business must have extremely low transactional costs, ideally with no commissions and no brokerage charges.

14. **Can use leverage, allowing business owner to use other people's money easily** - Leverage is the concept of being able to achieve a lot with a little. In business terms, it often implies using other people's money, rather than your own. This can be a very powerful feature, as it allows business owners to increase the size of their transactions quickly. However, using other people's money can often be very expensive and requires a great deal of administration and red tape. In our perfect business, the choice of using leverage must be available to us, but it must be available instantly, without requiring lengthy administration forms to complete and be very inexpensive.

15. **Completely level playing field; no advantages to people with larger bank balances** - As any business owner knows, competition can be a good thing. It can inspire innovation and progress. However, it can also create challenges to new entrants into the market. Those people with more money may be able to manipulate markets or suppliers to

give themselves an advantage. While this is very true in traditional businesses, our perfect business must provide the same opportunity and risk/reward potential to all participants, thus giving new entrants a fair chance to succeed.

16. **Little time required to run the business; 10-60 minutes a day maximum** - We live in the information age. In the previous industrial and agricultural ages, it was necessary for people to spend their time working in order to receive a return. Today, it's possible to conduct transactions effortlessly, wirelessly, electronically, instantly. Generating a return must not be a result of having to spend a lot of time performing an activity. Instead, our perfect business must allow us to potentially generate unlimited returns without having to spend more than an hour a day focusing our attention on our business.

17. **Easy to learn, easy to do** - Many traditional and even modern businesses require a great deal of specific expertise which can take years of training. Our perfect business must be easy to learn and easy to implement requiring, at most, a few days of training in order to get started. Like any business, though, with practice will come experience, and our perfect business will allow us to improve our confidence and skill with practice.

18. **Excellent training, support and guidance from highly experienced professionals available** - Our perfect business may be easy to do, but that also depends on the training we receive. You've no doubt heard that the best way to learn to do something well is to find someone else who is already an expert at it, and then do the exact thing. Therefore, we must have access to comprehensive, easy to learn training and more importantly, outstanding support and guidance from highly experienced professionals.

FOREX TRADING

I'm sure you would agree that a business that could meet all of these criteria would be a very exciting and interesting business opportunity! A business opportunity which would demand a much closer inspection.

Does such a business actually exist?

Well, not only does it exist, but it's been going on for years! It's the largest market in the world and guess what? You've already participated in it, many times over!

It's the **FOREIGN EXCHANGE** market, or **FOREX** for short. In other words, currency trading.

Let's go through the basics of how it works…

THE BASICS
The Foreign Exchange (FOREX) market is the largest market in the world, turning over more than $4 trillion per day and growing!

Forex is simply the practice of exchanging one currency for another. For example, you may have visited a foreign country, and you no doubt exchanged your native country's currency for the local currency, in order to have some spending money in your pocket.

Alternatively, you may have purchased something online from overseas, and you used your credit card to pay for the goods. Your bank would have converted your local currency into the foreign currency in order to complete the financial transaction. Either way, you have participated in the Forex market.

The Forex market is a worldwide, decentralised financial market for trading currencies. The market is open 24 hours a day, with the exception of weekends.

Currency values differ between nations due to various economical, political and social influences. The Forex market allows buyers and sellers to come together to exchange currencies and ultimately determine the relative values of the different currencies.

Prior to the modern Forex market, which began forming in the early 1970s, the world did not have floating currency values. Instead, a system known as the Bretton Woods Agreement was the monetary system since the end of World War Two (WWII).

HISTORY OF THE FOREX MARKET
Following WWII, Europe, Russia and Japan were in financial and physical ruin. The United States emerged as the wealthiest and most powerful nation on Earth. In fact, one of the reasons which lead to WWII was an unstable monetary system causing high inflation and wildly fluctuating currency values. In an effort to provide a stable platform for post-war nations to rebuild, the Bretton Woods Agreement was entered into by all the major nations in 1945.

The Bretton Woods Agreement set out the following conditions:

- gold would be fixed at $35 USD an ounce;

- the US Dollar (USD) would be backed by physical gold, that is, in order to print more USD, the United States had to have more gold in storage;

- other nations' currencies, such as the Great British Pound, the Japanese Yen and the German Deutschmark were all fixed (pegged) to the US dollar, and only allowed to fluctuate in value a maximum of plus or minus one per cent;

- all major commodities such as gold, crude oil, copper, wheat, silver etc. were all to be priced in US dollars.

All of this meant that the US Dollar became the Global Reserve Currency. (A Reserve currency is a currency that is held in significant quantities by governments and institutions around the world). Prior to WWII, the Great British Pound was the Global Reserve Currency. This provided a massive advantage to the United States.

The Bretton Woods Agreement did prove successful in keeping inflation low and allowing international financial transactions and investments to occur, which, in turn, provided nations the time and stability they needed to recover from the war.

However, during the 1950s, 1960s and 1970s the United States started to abuse their position of power. They printed far more US dollars than they were allowed to, to help pay for various expenses and wars such as the Korean and Vietnam wars, as well as their nuclear weapons program and the Cold War.

At the same time, Germany, Japan and other nations had sufficiently recovered and did not appreciate the United States' abuse of power.

A run on the Gold Market commenced, which lead President Richard Nixon to terminate the Bretton Woods Agreement in 1971. This act abolished the Gold Standard, meaning that the US Dollar was no longer backed by gold.

However, the US Dollar remained the Global Reserve Currency, and to this day, commodities are still priced in US Dollars. This still provides the United States with a significant advantage, as nations must convert their currency to US Dollars in order to purchase commodities. This creates an artificial demand for the US Dollar, thereby providing strength for the value of the US Dollar.

In 1973 the modern day Forex market replaced the Bretton Woods Agreement, allowing the major nation's currencies to freely float and fluctuate. This has resulted in wildly fluctuating currency values over the past 40 years, as well as volatile levels of inflation, but it has also created the most exciting market place where anyone can have access to a state-of-the art business opportunity.

THE MAJOR CURRENCIES
One aspect that makes trading currencies relatively simple and popular is that there are very few currencies to consider. While every nation on Earth has their own currency, when it comes to trading currencies as a business, traders focus on only six to 10 different currencies.

Compare that to the US stock markets, where there are more than 6,000 publicly traded companies, or to real estate where there are literally millions upon millions of different properties. You can see how simple Forex can be when you only have to consider a handful of currencies.

FOREX TRADING

The major currencies (and their percentage of global reserves):

USD – United States Dollar (60%)

EUR – Euro (23%)

JPY – Japanese Yen (5%)

GBP – Great British Pound (5%)

All other currencies in the world make up only 7% of all currencies!

CAD – Canadian Dollar   AUD – Australian Dollar

NZD – New Zealand Dollar   CHF – Swiss Franc

NOK – Norwegian Krone   SEK – Swedish Krona

The naming system for currencies is also quite simple. The first two letters of the three letter code denote the country e.g. AU for Australia, US for United States, NZ for New Zealand. The third letter of the code denotes the type of currency, such as D for dollars, Y for Yen, K for Krone and F for Franc.

The Swiss Franc is the trickiest, as CH stands for Confoederatio Helvetica (Latin is used due to the quadrilingual population).

EASE OF TRADING
Forex trading may seem quite complicated and challenging, but once you understand some basic principles, you'll be surprised by how simple it can be.

Before we can understand Forex, it's important to understand economies.

There are two main types of economies in the world:

1. **Commodity-based economies** - These are economies where the majority of the Gross Domestic Product (GDP), or the overall revenue of the country, is derived from the mining and production of commodities (oil, wheat, gold, lumber, livestock etc).

2. **Manufacturing and services-based economies** - These are economies where the majority of the GDP or overall revenue of the country is derived from manufacturing goods and or providing services.

Take Australia as an example. Australia has thriving manufacturing and services industries; however, the overwhelming majority of GDP for Australia comes from the mining of a wide variety of commodities. Hence, Australia would be considered a commodity-based economy.

Japan's economy, by comparison, is heavily geared towards manufacturing such as vehicles, computers, appliances etc. As Japan is such a physically small country with a large population, they produce very few commodities and hence have to import virtually everything they need, such as iron ore, oil, wheat etc. Japan is therefore considered a manufacturing-based economy.

The United States is a juggernaut when it comes to production of commodities, with significant oil, gold, and wheat production. However, their manufacturing and services industries are larger yet again, making the United States known as a manufacturing and services-based economy.

FOREX TRADING

Commodity-based economies	Manufacturing and services-based economies
AUD	USD
CAD	EUR
NZD	JPY
NOK	GBP
SEK	CHF

FORCES WHICH INFLUENCE VALUES

There are many different forces which continually interact to establish the spot (up to the second) currency value, however, it all boils down to supply and demand. If there is a greater demand (less supply) for a particular currency, then its value will increase. A falling demand (greater supply) will result in a falling currency value.

One very interesting aspect to currency trading as a business is to realise that approximately 70 to 80 per cent of all daily currency transactions are not being made to make a profit. Instead, the majority of currency exchange transactions are being conducted to allow for international trade and investment.

For example, let's assume that a clothing business in Australia purchases $500,000 USD worth of material from a supplier in the United States. The Australian business must pay the US business in USD, but they only have AUD in their bank account. They would have to contact their bank and have the bank convert their AUD into USD at the current exchange rate and send it to the supplier's account.

The Australian business has just participated in the Forex market, but they didn't do it to make a profit from exchanging the currency. Rather, they simply had to exchange their currency into a currency that the supplier would accept.

Or when international travellers require local currency for spending money. They exchange their currency at a Bureau de Change (currency exchange office) usually found at airports and tourist hotspots. The travellers aren't exchanging their currency to make a profit (in fact, they know they are usually being ripped off!). They simply have the need for local currency.

The overwhelming majority of daily currency transactions are conducted this way - not for profit, but for necessity.

What we are discussing in this chapter is the business of specifically trying to make a profit from exchanging one currency for another, and then back again. Interestingly, only approximately 20 to 30 per cent of all transactions have this as their desired outcome.

Compare this to the stock market, where virtually every transaction is conducted with profit being a goal. Whether it's an investor buying the shares for the long term, or a short-term speculator, or one corporation trying to take over another one, all the transactions are being conducted with the focus on making a profit at some point in the future.

This is an important distinction, as it helps to understand the motivations behind the market, and therefore helps to identify the forces of supply and demand.

Despite all the transactions occurring every day, there are only two main forces which really affect currency values: **Commodity Prices** and **Interest Rates**.

FOREX TRADING

COMMODITY PRICES

The most important trading commodity in the world is crude Oil. Every industry in the world depends on energy, whether that's in the form of petrol, diesel or jet fuel. All three are derived from crude oil.

And every commodity in the world needs energy to produce, mine or farm it. For example, digging gold out of the ground requires a huge amount of energy, and of course, then there is the transportation of the gold to the final destination.

Therefore, if the price of crude oil rises, then the production and transportation costs of every commodity must rise. These costs are then passed on to the end consumer.

If commodity prices are rising then that is considered **STRENGTH** for commodity-based currencies, such as the AUD, CAD, and NZD. Those currencies will likely experience a rise in their values.

Conversely, that is considered **WEAKNESS** for manufacturing-based currencies, such as the JPY, USD, GBP. Those currencies will likely experience a fall in their values.

If commodity prices are falling, then that is considered **WEAKNESS** for commodity-based currencies, and **STRENGTH** for manufacturing-based currencies.

INTEREST RATES

Every day, trillions of dollars around the world are invested seeking a return. If one nation offers a higher interest rate than another, then investors are incentivised to exchange their currency for the other in order to receive a better rate of interest.

This in turn creates a demand for the currency, hence providing **STRENGTH** for that currency's value.

Therefore, if interest rates are rising (or even suspected of rising) then that is considered **STRENGTH** for that particular nation's currency. The currency value will likely rise.

If interest rates are falling (or even suspected of falling) then that is considered **WEAKNESS** for that particular nation's currency. The currency value will likely fall.

TRADING ONE CURRENCY AGAINST ANOTHER
The business of currency trading involves exchanging one currency for another, and then back again at a later date.

The goal is to exchange one currency when it is at a low value compared to the other currency, and then exchange it back when it's at a higher value. The difference between the two values becomes the trader's return (either profit or loss).

When trading currencies, we always compare the value of one currency against another. Therefore, think of currency trading like a see-saw:

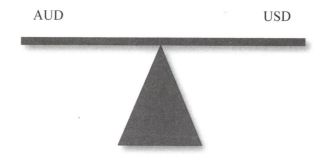

FOREX TRADING

If commodity prices are rising, then a commodity-based currency will likely rise against a manufacturing-based currency:

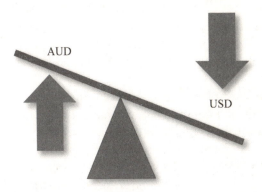

Let's now see how these forces have influenced the interaction between the AUD and the USD over the past 17 years...

1995-2000

Between 1995 to 2000, the United States' stock markets experienced what was known as the **"Tech Boom"**.

The value of the S&P500 Index (the top 500 USA stocks) rose by more than 150 per cent! The value of the NASDAQ index (mainly technology stocks) rose by more than 400 per cent!

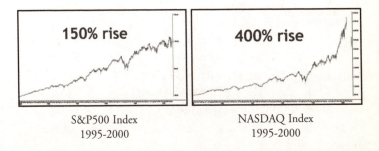

S&P500 Index
1995-2000

NASDAQ Index
1995-2000

The massive rally in US stocks created a huge demand from international investors, who all wanted to buy US stocks. Therefore, they had to convert their international currencies into USD in order to buy the US stocks.

This created an enormous demand for the USD.

And as a result of the strong economy in the US, the Federal Reserve (the US Central Bank commonly known as the FED) increased interest rates by approximately two per cent. At the same time, demand for commodities was at an extreme low!

Gold traded at a low of $250/oz (a 20-year low price), crude oil traded at a low of only $10/barrel, and copper traded at a low of only $0.60 per pound, just to name a few!

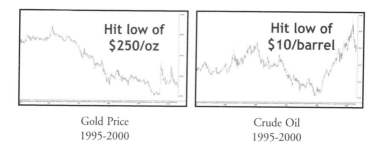

Gold Price
1995-2000

Crude Oil
1995-2000

The Australian economy was struggling due to the extremely low commodity prices so the Reserve Bank of Australia (RBA) lowered the Australian interest rates by more than two per cent.

Therefore, with massive STRENGTH of the USD, and a lot of WEAKNESS for the AUD, the AUD fell to only $0.50 against the USD by 2000, the lowest level it had ever been! In fact, the value of the AUD was so low that it was commonly referred to as the "Pacific Peso".

FOREX TRADING

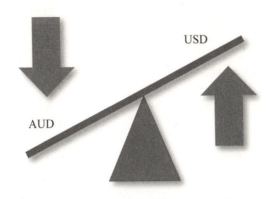

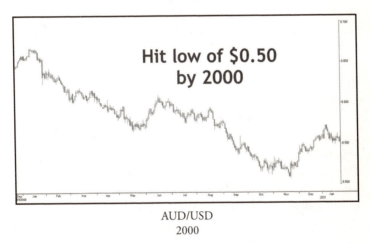

AUD/USD
2000

However, by late 2000, things started to completely reverse...

2000-2003

By early 2000, the Tech Boom quickly became the **"Tech Crash"**. The fantastic rise in stock values could not continue, and once investors started to sell down their stocks, the market fell extremely quickly. By the end of 2000, the NASDAQ Index had lost more than 50 per cent of its value!

DANIEL KERTCHER

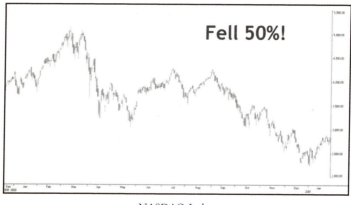

NASDAQ Index
2000

Then, just as the Tech Crash was bottoming out in late 2001, the United States was attacked on 11 September 2001. The stock market fell more than 20 per cent over the following two weeks. It completely recovered within a month, but the feelings of personal and national security by both Americans and citizens around the world were forever shattered.

Then in April 2002, not even a year following the 9/11 disaster, Enron and WorldCom became the two biggest corporate collapses in US history (up to that point in time). The stock market lost more than 40 per cent of its value in the following four months!

FOREX TRADING

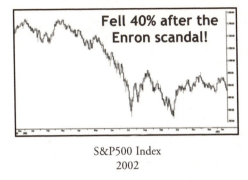

S&P500 Index
2002

In an effort to help the now struggling US economy, the FED dropped interest rates to an unprecedented one per cent per annum, the lowest US interest rate in 55 years. Remember, that is weakness for their currency value.

Following the attacks of 9/11, the United States, along with Great Britain, Australia and other countries, began their preparations for the invasion of Iraq. As Iraq has some of the largest oil deposits of any country in the world, the price of oil quickly started to rise. And if oil rises, other commodities follow suit.

By 2003, the crude oil price had surged more than 50 per cent and gold had risen more than 25 per cent in value. That is strength for commodity-based currencies.

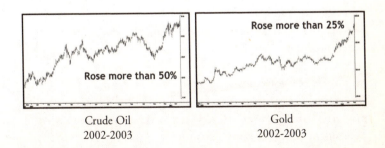

Crude Oil
2002-2003

Gold
2002-2003

Due to rising commodity prices and the subsequently improving Australian economy, the Australian RBA had to raise Australian interest rates. They increased the rates by more than two per cent (strength for their currency value).

So, with significant weakness for the USD and strength for the AUD, it's not surprising that the AUD rose more than 62 per cent against the USD to a high of $0.78 in just over a year.

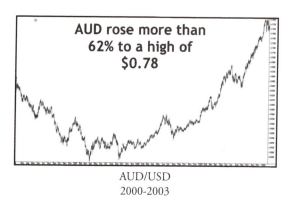

AUD/USD
2000-2003

2004-2006

In 2002, in an effort to allow low income and even no income earners an opportunity to acquire a home and mortgage, the lending qualifications were substantially lowered, both in the United States and Australia. New mortgages, known as "Sub-Prime" Loans became widely available. In Australia, these were known as "Low Doc" or "No Doc" loans.

Hundreds of thousands of new loans were created, and if you lend money to people, they are going to spend it. As a result, property prices started to skyrocket. This practice, and the subsequent property boom, continued until July 2007.

FOREX TRADING

And as property values rose, homeowners refinanced their mortgages in order to draw out equity in order to spend on other investments and consumer items (cars, holidays, appliances etc).

The stock markets around the world (especially in Australia and the United States) boomed!

And due to the continued wars in Iraq and Afghanistan, commodity prices continued to set new record highs.

Both the FED and the RBA increased interest rates in order to keep the two economies under control and avoid runaway inflation.

So, with strength for both currencies occurring at the same time, the AUD basically tracked sideways against the USD for much of 2004 to 2006.

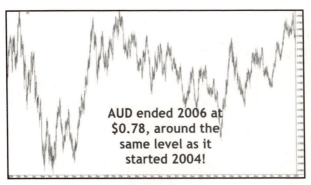

AUD/USD
2004-2006

2007-2008

By July 2007, the housing market in the United States essentially ran out of new home owners. Everyone who wanted a mortgage by that point had one. And with rising interest rates due to the booming economy, many of the Sub-Prime loan clients could no longer afford their mortgages. Foreclosures, which were previously a trickle, turned into a flood. By late 2007, the Sub-Prime Crisis was a household phrase around the world.

Property prices collapsed, losing more than 30 per cent in national average across the United States.

With property prices falling, confidence in the stock markets quickly eroded. Stock indices started to fall for the first time in four years.

But despite the falling property and stock values, commodities continued to rally, fuelled by the ongoing Middle Eastern wars as well as China's insatiable demand for raw materials for their ambitious urbanisation programs.

The crude oil price hit a high of $148 /barrel in mid 2008. That's a rise of more than 1,300 per cent in only eight years. The gold price reached $1,000/oz, an all-time record high.

FOREX TRADING

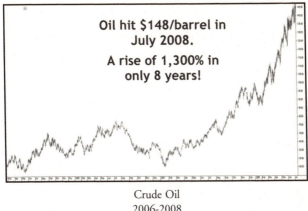

Crude Oil
2006-2008

Faced with hundreds of thousands of foreclosures, and the prospect of millions more, and despite the highest inflation levels since 1990, the FED lowered interest rates to one per cent, a multi-decade low.

Meanwhile, the RBA increased the Australian interest rates to counteract the stratospheric commodity prices.

These events created massive strength for the AUD against the USD. The AUD rallied more than 44 per cent to $0.98 against the USD, the highest level since the currency was first floated.

The days of calling the Australian dollar the "Pacific Peso" seemed to be over. It was now worth almost the same as the US dollar!

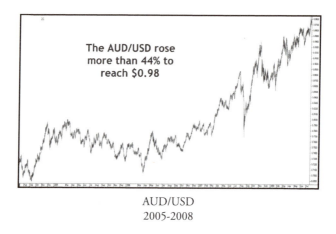

AUD/USD
2005-2008

By mid 2008, a series of major US companies announced terminal liquidity issues and began to file for bankruptcy - AIG, General Motors, Bear Stearns, Lehman Brothers, and more. Confidence in the stock market plummeted, resulting in the S&P 500 losing more than 43 per cent of its value - the biggest stock market crash of the past 80 years!

S&P 500 Index
2008

USA National Average
Real Estate Index
2007-2008

Faced with massive losses in real estate (The USA National Average Real Estate Index showed that average prices across America fell by more than 60 per cent from 2007-2009), dwindling stock values and investor confidence at record lows,

FOREX TRADING

institutions were forced to liquidate their profitable commodity holdings, in order to reallocate their funds and cover their losses. This action prompted the largest commodity price collapse in history.

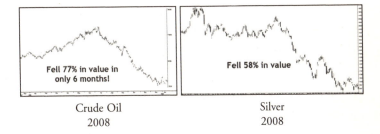

| Crude Oil | Silver |
| 2008 | 2008 |

Crude oil fell from $148/barrel to only $32/barrel in only six months, the biggest drop for the oil price in history. That meant that crude oil was trading down at its production costs. Virtually every other commodity on Earth also fell to their production costs: gold fell to $700/oz, silver fell to $8.50/oz and copper fell to $1.30 per pound.

Unlike stocks, which can fall to $0 if the company goes bankrupt, commodity values cannot fall to $0, as there is a production cost to every commodity. It costs money to produce commodities (wages, energy, exploration etc). Therefore, if commodities are trading at their production costs, then that is effectively the lowest the commodity prices will go, because if commodity prices fell below production costs, the producers would simply stop production. The resultant drop in supply would drive the price back up again.

The domino effect of the real estate market collapse, followed by the stock market collapse and the commodity market collapse turned the Sub-Prime Crisis into the Global Financial Crisis (GFC).

Countries around the world all dropped their interest rates to record lows in an attempt to keep money flowing in the economy and prevent a total capital freeze, which would have resulted in catastrophic job losses and complete financial meltdown.

The US interest rates were dropped to 0.25 per cent, the lowest level in US history. The Australian rates were dropped to three per cent, still the highest of any major nation around the world, but the lowest rates Australia had seen in 60 years.

Overall, real estate, stocks and commodities had all lost more than 50 per cent of their values in less than one year.

Institutions, governments, individual investors all sold their various investment holdings in the greatest sell-off the world had seen since the Great Depression.

But with so many people selling, they raised an enormous amount of cash. The question then became, "Where would they all place the cash?"

Well, there are only four main areas to invest cash, and it's the same for large institutions, corporations and fund managers as it is for any individual investor.

People can invest their money into:

- Real estate
- Stock market
- Commodities
- Bank (Term Deposit) or Bonds.

Real estate, stocks and commodities were all being sold off, creating massive amounts of cash which needed to be invested; the only place left was the bank (Bonds).

FOREX TRADING

Small individual investors would likely deposit their money into a bank's term deposit for safe keeping, but large institutions, governments, corporations and high net worth investors prefer to invest their money into bonds.

Bonds are basically a loan - you loan your money to someone else and at some point in the future you will receive your money back, with interest.

US government bonds, despite the problems with the US economy, were seen as the safest bonds in the world, as they were backed by the US government, considered one of the most stable and wealthiest in the world.

Investors around the world poured billions of dollars into US 20-year Treasury Bonds.

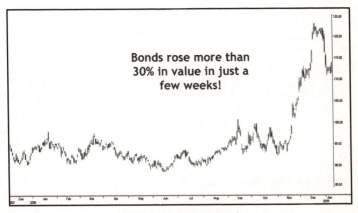

US 20-Year Treasury Bonds
2008-2009

In order to buy US Bonds, international investors had to convert their currency into US dollars. This created a massive demand for the US dollar.

So despite the real estate, stock and commodity markets all crashing in value, as well as plummeting interest rates, the US dollar demand was extremely high. At the same time, the AUD lost all its strength as the commodity prices collapsed.

As a consequence, the AUD had one of its biggest falls against the USD in history, falling 40 per cent in value in only three months. It took the AUD five years to rise from $0.61 to $0.98, but only three months to fall back to $0.61 again!

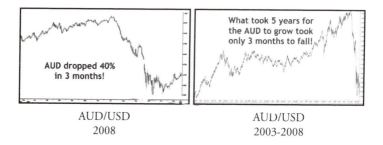

AUD/USD
2008

AUD/USD
2003-2008

2009-2012

By early 2009, the Global Financial Crisis was in full swing. Stocks, real estate and commodities were at decade-low prices, and bonds were at all-time high prices, earning the lowest interest rate returns in history.

How long would you expect investors to leave money in bonds receiving record low returns? Not very long at all! But at the time, investors weren't concerned about a "Return **on** Capital", instead, they were worried about a "Return **of** Capital". They only had their money in bonds as a safe haven, somewhere they knew they wouldn't lose their money.

But by March 2009, the stock and commodity markets seemed to be bottoming out. Commodities couldn't go any lower as

FOREX TRADING

they had reached their production costs level, meaning that if prices fell any further, commodity producers would have stopped production, thereby driving up prices by limiting the supply.

Investors started to pull their money back out of the bond market, evidenced by the rapid drop in the bond market prices.

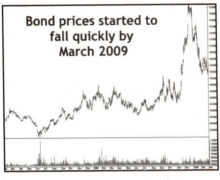

US 20-Year Treasury Bonds
2008-2009

With money obviously coming out of the bond market, the big question became, "Where is the money going to go?"

Would it go back into real estate? Absolutely not! The US foreclosure rate was still skyrocketing and banks were refusing to lend money for mortgages in most cases. It would take many years for the US real estate market to recover, not just a few months.

What about the stock market? Well, at the time the US Congress was conducting publicly televised hearings with many of the top 500 company CEOs, asking them to explain why the GFC had happened. The CEOs from General Motors, Ford and Chrysler all went to Washington demanding bailout packages. Richard

Fuld, the CEO from Lehman Brothers, one of the largest investment banking companies which collapsed, had to defend why he personally received in excess of $200 million while his company went bankrupt, his employees became jobless and the shareholders lost their investment.

And to make matters worse, when the bailout money was sent to companies like AIG, they used some of the proceeds to pay out bonuses to their executives!

It's easy to see why investors had virtually no confidence in the stock market nor the CEOs running the businesses. Therefore the money coming out of the bond market was not likely to be flooding back into the stock market.

So, that only left one sector - commodities!

Commodities were an obvious choice for investors for many reasons. Firstly, despite the global recession, there was still a very strong demand for commodities. The world continued to consume crude oil, iron ore, silver, wheat etc. The global economy may have slowed down, but it didn't stop all together. People still travelled to work, still ate food, still consumed.

Secondly, commodities as an investment had some advantages. Commodities couldn't go bankrupt, like a company could. Commodities didn't need bailouts, like some companies did. Commodities were tangible, something physical and, in times of high uncertainty, investors like to invest in things that they can touch.

And seeing as commodities such as crude oil were trading at their production costs, it was almost impossible for the price to fall further, as producers would have simply stopped production,

FOREX TRADING

in turn reducing supply and ultimately driving the price back up again.

And as we know, a rising commodity market would translate into a healthier Australian economy, where the Reserve Bank of Australia would likely increase interest rates. This would be obvious strength for the value of the Australian Dollar.

My view was that commodities were going to rise as money came back out of the bond market and went looking for a home. As commodity values rose, the AUD would also rise against the USD.

In fact, I was so certain of this chain of events that I conducted live seminars in front of thousands of people all around Australia teaching them how to buy gold and crude oil.

I even produced DVDs, explaining the same strategies, which we distributed internationally.

But for those people who really understood what I was talking about, who could see the fantastic potential opportunity in the market, I taught them how to trade Forex, specifically, the AUD versus the USD.

TRADING FOREX
Trading Forex is actually quite a simple procedure. First of all, you need to open an account with a reputable Forex broker. I use a firm known as Spectrum Live, whom I've been a client of since 2005. They are highly professional, use an award-winning online platform which is especially good for Forex trading, and have very competitive rates.

Let's go through an example:

Let's say that you wish to purchase $100,000 worth of AUD against the USD. With Forex trading, you don't invest the full amount yourself. Instead, you only require a small fraction of the full value (known as the **Face Value**).

Most brokers, including Spectrum Live, require a margin of one per cent. That is, you need to have one per cent of the face value in your account.

One per cent of $100,000 (face value) is equal to $1,000.

Therefore, to buy $100,000 worth of AUD versus USD in your account, the broker will require you to provide $1,000. The amount that you are providing is known as **Margin**.

This now means that you are controlling one hundred times more money in the market than you have invested yourself. You therefore have a leverage ratio of 1:100. In other words, every one per cent the currency value moves in your favour, you will make 100 per cent profit!

If the currency moves 10 per cent in your favour, you will make 1,000 per cent profit!

However, it's critical to understand that the currency price could move in the opposite direction. Every one per cent the currency value moves against you will result in a 100 per cent loss!

If the currency price moves 10 per cent against you, then you will lose 1,000 per cent, or 10 times your margin!

FOREX TRADING

> Forex trading can generate spectacular profits, hence why it is such a popular instrument to trade. But it can also result in enormous losses. Downside risk protection is therefore critical! We will discuss risk management in the next section.

Let's now discuss the AUD/USD trade I made back in March 2009.

Once I identified the global financial movements, and could see that billions of dollars were flooding out of the bonds market and would likely go into the commodities market, I decided to buy AUD against the USD.

Let's assume I purchased $100,000 AUD/USD (in reality I purchased more, but this will keep things simple).

I provided my $1,000 margin (one per cent of the face value) and purchased the AUD/USD at $0.68 in March 2009.

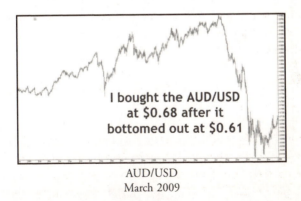

AUD/USD
March 2009

Over the next three years, by 2012, my view proved to be correct. The price of gold rose more than 150 per cent and the price of crude oil rose more than 220 per cent!

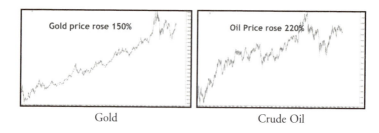

Gold   Crude Oil

As the commodity prices rose, the Reserve Bank of Australia (RBA) increased the Australian interest rates from three to 4.75 per cent. Meanwhile, the FED kept the US interest rates at the all-time low of 0.25 per cent.

The combined rise in commodity prices and Australian interest rates resulted in the AUD rising to an all-time high of $1.10 against the USD by August 2011, a rise of 61 per cent since my entry at $0.68 in March 2009.

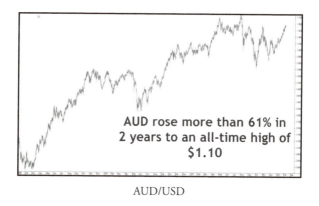

AUD/USD

A rise of 61 per cent might not sound as exciting as a rise of 150 per cent such as gold, or 220 per cent such as oil, but don't forget, Forex trading has the benefit of 100 times leverage!

FOREX TRADING

That means that my trade made 61 per cent x 100 = 6,100 per cent profit!

On an investment of $1,000 margin, a profit of 6,100 per cent resulted in $61,000 profit!

Ask yourself, did you have $1,000 you could have risked on the AUD/USD back in March 2009? If you had done the same trade as I did, you would have made $61,000 profit!

A $10,000 investment would have made a profit of $610,000!

As you can see, Forex trading can generate huge returns if the trade goes in your favour.

It's important to remember too though, that if the trade had gone against us, 100 times leverage can result in huge losses! If the currency had fallen 10 per cent in value, we would have lost 1,000 per cent. So, it's critical to manage risk, which we will discuss in the next section.

INTEREST INCOME
In addition to the capital gain profit, the trade also made me an income of 400 per cent interest per year on my margin capital. On $1,000 margin, that's an income of $4,000 per year, paid daily, into our account - even including weekends!

An income of 400 per cent interest per year on the margin capital? How is that possible?

Well, when you trade currencies, you earn interest on the currency you are buying, while you pay interest on the counter currency.

In this case, the Australian interest rates hit a high of 4.75 per cent. That means that I was earning 4.75 per cent per year on the face value of the trade ($100,000). But I had to pay interest on the USD side of the trade, which was 0.25 per cent.

The broker also takes a cut for their fee, which is 0.5 per cent with the broker I use. This is a typical charge by all Forex brokers, as they don't charge commission on the trades.

    4.75% Australian interest

    <u>-0.25%</u> USA interest

    4.50% Gross interest

    <u>-0.50%</u> Broker cut

    4.00% Net interest per year

Therefore, I earned four per cent net interest per year on $100,000, which equalled $4,000 income per year!

That money was credited into my account on a daily basis. That is, $11 per day ($4,000 divided by 365) was credited into my account, including weekends. The Saturday and Sunday interest payments went into my account on each Monday. What a great way to start a week!

Earning interest on your Forex trade is known as a **Positive Carry Trade**.

It's important to realise though, that if the interest rates were around that other way, that is, the Australian interest rates were lower than the US interest rates, I would have had to pay out interest on this trade, plus the broker's cut.

FOREX TRADING

When you have to pay out interest on a Forex trade, it's known as a **Negative Carry Trade**. It's therefore critical that you have an understanding of interest rates and their likely future direction before you enter a Forex trade.

Another wonderful feature of trading Forex is that at any time, we can close out (sell) any or all of our position. In fact, there are no brokerage charges when trading Forex. That is, the broker doesn't charge a commission when we trade. We simply have a price spread which is usually two to four pips (about 0.0002 to 0.0004 of a cent on each dollar traded). This means that a trade with a face value of $100,000 costs us approximately $20-$40 to enter and to exit. I'm sure you'd agree that that is a very inexpensive cost to deal. To sell a house worth $100,000 would cost many thousands of dollars!

This entire trade on the AUD/USD took me a grand total of a few seconds to place into the market back in March 2009. For the next two to three years, I didn't do anything at all, except watch the market and watch my account value grow!

This is how we trade Forex. We don't sit in front of a computer for hours a day, buying and selling within minutes, becoming very stressed, and have no idea of what is actually driving the markets.

Instead, we patiently look for currency pairs which are stretched and trading at an extreme level, where they are likely to rebound as economic forces shift.

This particular trade was very obvious to me at the time, as I used a top-down, global approach to understanding the market. I wasn't looking at intra-day charts. I wasn't day trading.

Instead, I took the time to study the international markets - real estate, commodities, stocks, and bonds - and I combined my knowledge of international economics to identify the likely movement of money in the market. My view led me to realise that the AUD would likely rise substantially against the USD.

I applied my view by trading the AUD/USD, and over the next couple of years, my trade made me a fantastic capital gain as well as an excellent daily income of interest.

You can now start to realise why so many people are so excited about Forex trading.

There is simply no other market in the world which allows you to control 100 times more money than you have, and be able to manage it online, from anywhere in the world - let alone be able to potentially experience both substantial capital gain and income simultaneously.

RISK MANAGEMENT
Trading Forex can provide fantastic rewards, but as discussed earlier, can result in enormous losses, much greater than your original margin capital.

Remember, every one per cent a trade goes against you, you will lose 100 per cent of your margin capital. If a trade moves 10 per cent against you, you will lose 1,000 per cent or 10 times your original margin capital.

Therefore, it is critical to have a well thought out, proven trading plan and very strong downside risk management.

There are a variety of things you can do to manage your risk.

FOREX TRADING

1. **Only trade with a maximum of one to five per cent of your trading capital per trade.**

   Let's say that you have $10,000 in your trading account and you place one per cent of your capital on a trade as margin.

   One per cent of $10,000 is $100. Therefore, you place $100 on a trade as margin. That allows you to control a trade with a face value of $100 x 100 leverage = $10,000.

   So, you are controlling a trade worth $10,000 but you have only placed one per cent or $100 of your own money on the trade.

   Let's now assume that the currency pair moves five per cent against you: you would lose 500 per cent of $100, or $500.

   A loss of $500 in your account would be a loss of five per cent of your total capital. You would still have $9,500 left to keep trading.

   We strongly suggest that when you start trading, that you only engage a maximum of one to five per cent of your trading capital on any one trade at any one time.

   Remember, it's more important to LEARN than it is to EARN when you first start trading Forex. We strongly recommend that you do not deviate from this guideline for at least the first year of trading, or until you are completely confident that you understand the risks of trading Forex.

2. **Only have a maximum of two to five trades running at any one time.**

   Seeing as there are only six to eight major currencies worth trading, and they are split between commodity-based economies and manufacturing-based economies, there is no point in having any more than two to five trades running at any one time. This helps keep your trading simple and easy to manage.

3. **Use Forex Options to minimise risk.**

   Forex Options are excellent tools to substantially reduce risk while trading Forex.

   Options allow you to still enjoy unlimited upside potential profits while limiting downside risk.

   Basically, there are two types of Options - Calls and Puts.

   Call options give you the right to buy Forex and Put options give you the right to sell Forex.

   Let's say that you believe a Forex price is going to rise. Rather than buy the Forex currency pair as described above where you put down an initial margin amount and control 100 times more money in the market, you instead purchase a Call option on the Forex currency pair.

   The option will expire some time in the future, and you can decide how long you have before your option expires, up to one year. During the life of the option, if the currency pair moves in your favour, you will enjoy an excellent profit. However, if the currency pair moves against you, you cannot

FOREX TRADING

lose anymore than the price of the option; that is, 100 per cent of your investment capital.

Now, losing 100 per cent of your investment capital may sound like a high risk, but when compared to potentially losing many more times that with regular Forex, 100 per cent loss is much more attractive. And if you only invest an amount you can comfortably lose (as little as $50 per trade) you can manage your risk safely regardless of what happens in the market.

Another very powerful way to use options is to use them as **Insurance** against a Forex trade.

Let's say that you decide to enter a trade on the AUD/USD Forex pair. You place down your one per cent margin. You can then purchase a Put option, which gives you the guaranteed right to be able to sell your Forex trade for the exact price as what you bought it at (an At-The-Money Put option) up until the option expires.

By doing this, you have eliminated any risk on the Forex trade, during the life of the Put option. The only risk you now face is the cost of the Put option. That cost is usually three per cent of the face value of the Forex trade for a six-month option.

This is just like buying car insurance. When you buy car insurance, you risk the value of your car and any other damage you do to someone else if you have an accident. But, by buying car insurance, you have eliminated your financial risk if you have an accident.

Your only cost (risk) is the cost of buying the car insurance.

This is the same with Put options.

When you buy a Forex trade, you risk your margin capital and a lot more if the trade moves against you. By buying an At-The-Money put option, you eliminate the risk on the Forex trade, meaning that you cannot lose one cent of your margin capital. The only risk you now face is the cost of the option itself.

If the Forex trade moves in your favour, the first three per cent movement is usually enough to recover your cost of the put option (insurance). After that, the upside movement is pure profit to you, leveraged 100 times.

If the Forex trade moves against you, the absolute most you can lose is the cost of the put option (insurance). That amount is fixed and is usually three per cent of the face value (300 per cent of your margin capital). If you have a Positive Carry Trade, the interest you earn can also help pay you back the cost of buying the put option (insurance).

Therefore, think of it like this: you risk a maximum of $3 for a potential of making an unlimited profit ($10-$30 or more).

You could risk a maximum of $300 for a potential of making $1,000 or more! Or risk $3,000 for a potential of making $10,000 or more.

That is a very sensible risk management approach.

There are many more risk management techniques, but using options as insurance is one of the best techniques to use to manage risk. Further risk management training

FOREX TRADING

is strongly recommended before starting to do live Forex trades.

OPEN AN ACCOUNT

To get started, you need a minimum of $1,000 to place into your own trading account. We don't recommend starting with less than this amount; $1,000 gives you sufficient capital to place a variety of trades and still maintain a large cash balance in your account.

Of course, once you have more experience, there is virtually no limit to the size of your account.

GREATEST BUSINESS IN THE WORLD!

Forex trading is, in my opinion, the greatest business opportunity in the world! What other business can you think of which offers the following advantages:

- Uses a high degree of leverage – safely – in any market environment (recession, booms etc)

- You have total control – no staff, no customers, no government red tape

- Totally liquid – you can have all your investment capital back in your personal bank account within two business days

- Trade as little as $1,000 to over a billion dollars!

- Market trades 24 hours a day, five days a week

- Totally portable – trade from your iPad, smartphone, computer, from anywhere in the world

- Excellent training and support available

- No brokerage commission, just a very small cost to deal

- When applying a medium to long-term, Big Picture approach, trading can take as little as a few minutes a day to manage.

I'm sure you would agree that Forex trading is certainly the best business opportunity!

Chapter 6
SELLING AND MARKETING INFORMATION ONLINE

"I love making products and profits out of thin air."

SEAN RASMUSSEN

PROFILE

SEAN RASMUSSEN

Sean Rasmussen is one of Australia's foremost affiliate marketers and has sold over $8.6 million of affiliate products online in only a few years.

In 2004, Sean was just another construction electrician who was stuck in the rut of making ends meet. He was $350,000 in debt and had a young family to support on just one income.

Sean decided that it was time to make a change. He set a two-year goal to become a full-time Internet marketer and earn over $10,000 per month. There was only one obstacle: he knew absolutely nothing about the Internet, let alone how to market online! He also had to hold down a 12-hour-a-day job to pay off debts while learning his new craft.

Starting with almost no knowledge about the Internet, Sean took only 23 months to achieve his goal, and establish himself as an up-and-coming Aussie affiliate marketer to be reckoned with. After making over $10,000 per month working part-time, Sean increased his sales by 80 per cent in his first month full-time online and took only three months to triple his earnings.

Sean's online business has since gone from strength to strength. By 2007 he was averaging over $60,000 *per week* in affiliate sales.

Sean attributes his success to his unrivalled passion and ethical upbringing by his honest parents. His integrity shines through in his marketing skills.

Sean now lives in Bunbury, Western Australia, on a 20-acre riverside property with his wife and two sons. His passions are travelling with his family and encouraging people to pursue their dreams.

SELLING AND MARKETING INFORMATION ONLINE

CREATING PRODUCTS AND PROFITS OUT OF THIN AIR: A $100K BUSINESS MODEL

Making products out of thin air might not initially sound very realistic. Making $100,000 per annum, or more, probably sounds even less likely.

The business model you're about to hear about will show you that it is indeed very possible. It's not only possible to earn this level of money out of thin air but it's also possible to do it by monetising something you are very interested in or even extremely passionate about. By breaking things down into digestible chunks in this chapter, you will start to see how feasible this type of business plan really is.

Furthermore, this system will also show you that you can create a system that generates income that is relatively passive. Most people would agree that passive income streams are the best sort of income streams to have!

WHAT DOES PASSIVE INCOME MEAN?

Passive income involves earning money without having to trade your time for money. Imagine this for a moment: what would it be like *not* having to toil over every dollar earned? Imagine making money while you're on vacation or while you're sleeping. How great would that be? Right now, there are more passive income opportunities than ever. With technological advances, this is only going to get even easier. The time to start capitalising on this type of business plan is right now.

$100K DOESN'T HAVE TO EQUATE TO HOURS WORKED TIMES HOURLY WAGE!

If we do the math on earning $100K in a year and you were able to work just 40 hours a week to make the money, you'd be making about $48 an hour for around 2,080-plus hours of work in the year.

Not everyone can earn $48 an hour. If you're only able to earn about $25 an hour, you'd be working about 4,000 hours to reach the goal of $100K in a year. But with only 8,760 hours in the year, who wants to work 4,000 hours or even 2,080 hours if you don't really have to?

After all, we need about 2,900 hours a year to dedicate to sleeping alone! Think about how much time you also spend walking the dog, showering, dealing with your mother-in-law, and all the other tasks that regularly eat up your time. No wonder it's so difficult to spend time smelling the roses and enjoying life!

If you sleep around 2,900 hours in a year and you work from 2,080 to 4,000 hours a year, there sure isn't a whole lot of time left to pursue your passions, is there?

Instead of working for $48 per hour for 40 hours a week how would you like to earn a fair bit of money without constant effort?

EARN "ROYALTIES"

Authors and actors are good examples of passive income earners. You can think of passive income a bit like royalties. If you set things up appropriately, you'll be able to receive money from something long after you've done the work. This business plan also shows you how to generate passive income without having to do all the work yourself and without having to peddle your wares constantly. This is because it is a system that does several things, such as lay groundwork that enables people to continually find you and buy from you without your constant input.

This model provides the foundation and it can involve implementing an outsourcing model that results in some of (or most of) the work being done by other people. If you think about the actor analogy again, imagine that you have a stunt actor or body double. Or in terms of the author example, you'll have a ghost writer who writes the book but puts your name on the cover.

SET YOUR OWN EARNING GOALS
You don't have to strive to make $100K per year this way – the dollar figure is just a number. You can pick the number that appeals to your personal wants or needs.

You could decide that you want to try to make an extra few hundred dollars a week, for a start. You could also strive for a goal above and beyond $100K once your business is established and running like a well-oiled machine on autopilot. The business model we are going to explore is one that you are going to be 100 per cent in control of. Some people implement this as a side line and others delve into it and turn it into their main income - their livelihood.

Building $100K business model does however take effort. Don't misunderstand and think that this is a get rich quick scheme - it's not. But this model does *not* require you to spend over 2,080 hours or 4,000 hours of your time to make that sort of money. One of the great things about this business model is that the hours you spend now on your business could create passive income streams that pay off for many years to come; a bit like re-runs of your favourite old TV shows that are keeping those actors in sports cars, flash houses, Botox, and younger trophy spouses!

OK, so how will you build your business model to create products and make money out of thin air? Well, the hottest commodity on earth right now is *information*, so why not use the Internet and create information products?

WAIT. WHAT?
Hopefully you didn't just hear screeching tyres or a big scratch of a record when you read that. Don't close the page on this idea before you get a chance to understand how it works. It's a fantastic concept for several reasons.

Yes, there are some online business scams out there but there are also a lot of really great ways to capitalise on the possibilities the Internet has brought to the entrepreneurial-minded. You don't have to be sneaky or underhanded. The business model we're exploring here is built on integrity and value. You can get rewarded for providing value to others and you can base it on something that benefits you, as well.

There has *never* been a better time to be an online entrepreneur. Let's explore many of the reasons here.

- You can create valuable products that people will happily pay for and many of them will probably send you *Thank You* emails or post positive testimonials online about your product. Every time there is a positive word-of-mouth about your product or your brand, it will help propel your success levels forward. The viral nature of the World Wide Web and Social Media works to the advantage of the entrepreneur in today's society.

- The Internet has made it very doable to set up a $100K business model (or pick your magic number) that pays you a significant return on your investment of time and/or money.

SELLING AND MARKETING INFORMATION ONLINE

You don't even have to be Microsoft's Bill Gates or Facebook's Mark Zuckerberg to do it.

- Your products could be so good, in fact, that your customers begin referring new customers to you. You then become known as an authority in your niche - whatever that niche is. No, you don't need to start a sweat shop in your basement or in your garage. You don't even have to pour thousands of dollars into starting this sort of business.

- Your business start-up costs can be quite low and your yield could be quite high. The great thing about this model is that you can, quite literally, cash in on your passion in life without major start-up costs.

- As you start making a bit of money from your efforts, you could then invest some of that profit further into your business, enabling you to grow it and enabling you to spend less time managing it (without sacrificing your income potential).

INFORMATION PRODUCTS

Information products are a rapidly growing field. They meet the needs of people seeking information and because they are delivered digitally, the business model is very manageable. This type of business is a great one for people who want a business with low overhead costs and for those with a goal of maximising their earning potential without setting up a complex company with a lot of staff members who expect full-time salaries. Because digital delivery methods work so efficiently, and are so cheap, this means that there is very little overhead to you, the business owner.

Are you worried that you don't have the skills to create digital products? That's okay. I'll cover that here as well. You don't need to be technically savvy to do this. You just need to leverage some coordination of talent (you'll learn how to do that later on here, too) and the great thing about this business is that it can help you make money with something you are interested in or are passionate about.

THE INFORMATION SUPER HIGHWAY

The web is called the information super highway for good reason. People use it to find out things. You can use this to your advantage by unleashing your inner expert and helping people find the information they are looking for.

Everyone has a topic they know more about than the average person. Your life thus far and your accumulation of experiences have created that knowledge. Sharing your knowledge in that topic can help other people who are interested. This could, by the way, snowball into a profitable business for you.

UNLOCKING YOUR INNER EXPERT

The $100K business model will involve you having digital information products created and then sold online. You will do this by unlocking your inner expert.

What are you passionate about in life? How great could it be if you could find a way to cash in on that passion?

Is there something that gets your juices flowing to the degree that you'd be thrilled if you could spend all of your free time pursuing it and talking about it to others? Chances are that this passion of yours is something you *could* become a true expert in - if money was not a stumbling block. If you could find a way to monetise that passion, wouldn't that be icing on the cake?

How happy would you be?

SELLING AND MARKETING INFORMATION ONLINE

Those countless hours spent sleeping, earning money, walking the dog, and so on are probably in the way of pursuing your passion as much as you want to. You can't outsource the sleeping or the dealing with the mother-in-law part (there's a thought!) but a little bit of effort expended on the right activities could build you a business that buys you something everyone wants - more time to do what we want. If you could earn more money you could quit your job or cut back your hours or quit spending half your weekend cleaning the house (because you can now afford to outsource that task to a cleaner).

Unlocking your inner expert can be done! Even better, it can be easily monetised with the Internet. The great thing about it is that it doesn't really feel all that much like work. As you work to monetise your passion, you're enjoying learning more about the topic as well as sharing it with others. This creates the sort of synergy that produces viral results.

Viral results help you generate more customers and more money. The Internet is viral in nature so it is the perfect tool to help you share your expertise with people who want it - people who are actively looking for the information you have.

Have you ever noticed that the most successful and happiest people in the world tend to be people who spend their time doing what they love and what they are passionate about? Some of them don't make much money at it and still feel successful and are perfectly happy. Some of them make a boatload of money at it and are also happy (funny about that!).

When you love something and are truly passionate about it, selling it becomes easy. Why? Because you are being genuine! There's no need to fake it until you make it or "pretend" to be genuine when you're doing something you love. People believe you because you believe in what you're saying and it's then a whole lot easier to believe in yourself. Success naturally follows.

I'll re-phrase that slightly to emphasise it:

> *When you are genuine and passionate in business, success will follow.*

This sort of business can create a whole new life for you. Or it could simply improve your existing life. Some people transition to creating information products as their full-time gig. The great thing is that it can produce full-time (or better) income without full-time hours.

WOULD YOU LOVE TO FORGET THE SNOOZE BUTTON EXISTS?

Are you someone who hits the snooze button too many times in the morning? If so, you might also be someone who feels that nagging dread in your stomach on Sunday nights because the weekend is over with and you have to go back to the daily grind that you're not all that thrilled with.

Most people who drag their feet in the morning have lost their zest. Why? Because they have to get up and do something that isn't necessarily their choice but is just what they *must* do. Most people in life aren't living their ideal life and that's why so many trudge through a good chunk of their life waiting for small glimpses of freedom, such as for a weekend or a holiday.

But when you're doing something you love on a continuous basis, you don't hit the snooze button on the alarm clock. Why? There are two reasons:

SELLING AND MARKETING INFORMATION ONLINE

1) You're going to wake up excited each day. You won't be dreading the morning commute, the office politics, and the next eight to 10 hours ahead of you.

2) You could get to a point in life where you are not going to *need* an alarm clock. If you run your own information products business, you won't have to rise at a specific time each day or live by a Monday to Friday nine-to-five schedule. This means there won't be any incessant buzzing in your ear, telling you to get up in the morning. The business model we're talking about doesn't have to happen on a nine-to-five schedule. You can make your own schedule.

You might not be able to quit your day job straight away. And you don't have to quit your day job if you don't really want to. But, if you want to try to monetise your passion, this is the sort of business that could easily become your full-time business (and it could be one that has part-time hours).

WHAT DOES SUCCESS MEAN TO YOU?

For some, it means financial freedom. For some it means that they are excited about what they do. For most people, success means being able to make their own choices. That means you can choose to work today or choose to take the day off. It means that when you're up for work at 6am, you're up because you want to be up and you want to be working. You love your work! There are a lot of freedoms that can come as a result of being in control of your financial destiny and living your life on your own terms.

You can choose to help others because you have the financial stability to do so. You can feel good about the money you earn because your product or service helps others. Success is freedom and freedom makes you feel successful.

FINDING YOUR PASSION

Some people faced with the question about what their passion is, and what they'd love to spend their time doing, find it to be an easy answer. They can answer the question in a heartbeat.

For others, they're just not sure and that's often because they are living their life on autopilot, just working for the weekends and waiting for their next vacation. They exist rather than really living. Taking a self-discovery trek could be very helpful.

Stop and think about it for a little while.

- What do you enjoy doing in your spare time?
- What topics get you so excited that they make you lose track of time?
- If money was no object and you did a job just because you loved it, what would that job involve? Animals, charity, technology, a hobby like fishing or hunting, boating, rugby, golf, natural health, fitness, movies, reading? There is an endless list of things to consider.

WHAT ARE YOU AN EXPERT AT? TURN IT INTO A PASSION

If you're not sure about your passion yet, what are you an expert at? Everyone is an expert at something - even if they're not totally passionate about it.

For example, even if you're not passionate about your current job, it has likely made you an expert on a topic that is some sort of specialised niche. Others may benefit from that information and be willing to pay for it. You can also parlay this into a business that you can *become* passionate about because it's something you do on your own terms (or you use it to make money because you're using it as a springboard into learning something you actually *are* passionate about).

SELLING AND MARKETING INFORMATION ONLINE

Even if you're someone who already earns a living doing what you're passionate about but you want to rev up your earning power, this business model is also for you.

Some people worry that if they turn their passion into an income-earner, it will make them lose interest because it will become their job. If you don't want to, you won't have to continually live and breathe that topic until it becomes a job. When you create information products you have the option to outsource some or most of the tasks, if that's what you want to do.

You can keep working at the bits that excite and motivate you and outsource the bits that you find to be difficult or tedious. Collaborating with people who have the right skills can help you reach your goals while having fun doing it.

The fact of the matter is that the Internet is filled with people who want to know things. By delivering what they want, you can create wealth for yourself and have fun doing it.

CREATING INFORMATION PRODUCTS AROUND YOUR PASSION

eBooks now outsell printed books on Amazon.com. That's pretty astonishing and a sure sign of the evolution of the human thirst for continuous knowledge and self-improvement. You can use this to your advantage.

People can read eBooks on their computer, on a tablet device such as an iPad or a Blackberry Playbook, an eReader such as a Kindle or Kobo, or even on their smartphone. Once people start using this technology, it often creates an insatiable thirst for more information.

eBooks are downloaded continually. The time when people expect to purchase a hardcopy book is no longer.

eBooks fulfil an instant need. A large chunk of people don't want to wait for something to arrive in the post. People also like the idea of not having to store piles of books in their home or to carry books with them when they're on the move. Electronic books fill an immediate need for learning, for entertainment, and for solving problems or self-improvement.

You might expect fiction readers to encompass the vast majority of people downloading eBooks, since eReaders are now so popular, but this isn't the case. Non-fiction books are very popular.

At one eBook/information product marketplace, called Clickbank (http://www.clickbank.com), the site sells an eBook somewhere in the world approximately every three seconds. They have paid out over a billion dollars in eBook earnings to publishers and their affiliates in the past 13-plus years.

Creating eBooks and delivering them digitally to people provides a vast world of opportunity for you. Once the groundwork is laid, it is a very easy business to manage.

eBooks are not difficult to create, they are easy to deliver via digital delivery methods, and they are a great first step in a successful and proven ascension business model (I will go over what this model is in detail) that you can capitalise on.

PROVIDE SOLUTIONS FOR PROBLEMS

The idea behind this business model is that you will help other people with your expert knowledge. When you unlock that inner expert, you unlock great earning potential. People are naturally attracted to experts and you can learn how to leverage the Internet to attract people who are interested in buying information products from you.

SELLING AND MARKETING INFORMATION ONLINE

Before you write an eBook, it's important to understand what motivates people to buy non-fiction eBooks. The three top reasons are:

1. It will help them save time

2. It will help them make or save money

3. They believe it will help make their life better.

People seek information from experts but they also actively seek solutions to their specific problems. Just look at the multi-billion dollar self-help industry!

Provide solutions to the problems people are looking to solve and you increase the chance that they will buy from you.

Do it well and they will buy more products from you.

Do it *exceptionally* well and they will tell other people about you, bringing you more earning potential. They might also tell people online about you in online places that will get you great attention.

How do you sell to people? You need to be where they look.

In this business model, you'll want to get very intimately acquainted with Google. Beyond using Google to find out information, you'll be using Google to help people find you and help instil the confidence in them that you are the right person to buy from.

Sometimes people look for an answer to a problem and when they find something that appears to fit the bill, they'll buy. They buy, most often, when the person presenting the solution appears believable and appears to be providing great value.

When the *pleasure* of the solution exceeds the *pain* of parting with the money, people will always buy.

Other times, people follow an expert for quite some time and when that expert presents a specific problem and a potential solution that appeals to that particular person, they will then buy. Some people require longer sales cycles than others and many people will buy repeatedly from someone who demonstrates ethics and good value. Building trusted relationships with as many people as possible is something that will serve you well.

Illustrate that you are a subject matter expert and that your eBook will help people with one of the three above areas and you could build a profitable business around that first step.

Google.com is going to be the tool that you leverage to help people find you. We are going to explore an **Ascension Model** that helps you attract people to buy products from you. You will use tools like Google, Facebook, Twitter, YouTube and other popular websites to help you get found, build relationships, and make money doing something you love.

OUTSOURCING: AN ASCENSION MODEL
Remember, in an earlier example, we talked about your ability

SELLING AND MARKETING INFORMATION ONLINE

to monetise your passion so that you wouldn't have to spend 2,080-plus hours earning $100K each year?

Effective outsourcing is one key to making this happen. If outsourcing is the key to the engine, then the **Ascension Model** is the fuel that will help you maximise profitability of your business.

START WITH AN IDEA
First, you need an idea. If that idea revolves around your passion or, at the very least, something you're really knowledgeable in, it's going to shave time and effort off the process.

Let's say for example, that you are someone who is passionate about health and wellness topics. You can't seem to get enough of learning about the latest super food, reading about truths about medicine, complimentary healing principles, healthy organic living, the latest in weight loss fad diets, and so on. This could be the passion you choose to monetise and it offers a wide breadth of possibilities.

Not only are you going to continually learn about the topic in your pursuit of implementing the business plan but this is a topic that is going to potentially help other people - like-minded people.

Just think of how many possible eBooks you could write around your topic! The world of health and wellness is a vast one and it's something that a vast number of people are interested in. Your eBook could be the start of your successful ascension model.

Or, if you're someone who loves boating and can't get enough of the topic, you could base your business around the love of boating. The people you attract might also be interested in other topics, such as fishing, the outdoors, and so on. You can create a profitable business around this topic that you're interested in and passionate about and it could expand into other relevant areas as time goes on.

WHAT'S AN ASCENSION MODEL?

An ascension marketing model involves multiple stages or tiers. With each stage, your profit-earning potential will increase.

It starts with attracting customers and serving a need of theirs. It then continues with developing a progressively positive relationship with them. Customers are attracted by an initial low-cost item that serves a need and then you continually build on a relationship of trust with them.

A permission-based marketing model is used to open the door to future communications. The relationship begins and it continues profitably. Marketing isn't just about advertising, it's about building a brand that becomes recognisable and desired. It's about relationships, too.

THE BENEFIT OF RELATIONSHIP MARKETING

Implementing a way to do relationship marketing is something that will be ongoing and after you've over-delivered on the initial eBook, you'll have a captive audience who is willing to entertain the idea of buying future items from you. You'll then take that opportunity to continue to demonstrate your expertise and provide valuable information to them. As this happens, you'll develop a symbiotic relationship. You'll provide something valuable and you'll get benefits in return, including potential sales, word-of-mouth referrals, and if you leverage social media sites like Facebook and others, you could benefit even further.

Once you open the door with someone and establish a relationship as a trusted advisor on the topic at hand, good things can happen.

SELLING AND MARKETING INFORMATION ONLINE

- That person becomes part of your online "tribe" and this provides social proof to others that you are an expert in your field. The nature of social media sites means that the more followers you have, the more others will see you as an authority and worth listening to.

- That individual buys more from you, often on a regular basis as your business grows, continually resulting in profits.

- That individual begins to refer others to you and refers to you as a go-to expert. Word-of-mouth marketing can be very powerful!

MORE ABOUT ONLINE TRIBES

An online tribe is a bit like an online entourage or posse. Relationship-building helps you build an online following that can be highly beneficial because people who follow you can buy from you and help you spread word-of-mouth about your brand. That online following helps you continually nurture existing and new relationships. Those relationships help you with your marketing efforts.

Sites like Facebook, Twitter, and other social media provide great opportunities for networking and establishing yourself as an authority to people who can become a captive audience. Creating online tribes offers great opportunities for getting found by potential customers. Using these tools will help you in many ways in your business model. We will explore ways to do this later on.

REPEAT BUYING

The key to success with your ascension model is that you're going to create a relationship with people that results in repeat buying behaviours. By providing value to people the first time they buy from you, you're going to increase the chances that they will spend money with you again and that they will take the plunge beyond the initial low-cost items.

ACHIEVING ONLINE EXPERT STATUS

Your relationship marketing efforts will result in you achieving an expert status so that instead of having to look for customers, people start to find you. This model doesn't just involve actively marketing to others but positions you in a way that results in people seeking you out. People who seek to find answers will naturally land on the places that you use as your online podiums.

Your presence can become so strong that you can quickly attain a status that means people trust you. Continue to drive your business forward with honesty, integrity, and passion and not only will you continually attract new sales but you'll have more freedom than ever to pursue the things in life you want to pursue - in business and in your personal life.

The ascension model is progressive. Again, you start with a low-cost item and establish a relationship and status as an authority on your subject. Then, you increase the chances that people will buy future products from you. Each of those products in the initial model is higher in price than the last. As you are selling products from multiple levels, your groundwork is in place, bringing new people into your sales funnel. The start of that sales funnel lies around your initial eBook.

CREATING A SALES FUNNEL

A sales funnel is a place where you can insert clients to walk them along a sales cycle. They enter the funnel as an interested potential client and leave the funnel when they buy something (but they don't leave permanently).

SELLING AND MARKETING INFORMATION ONLINE

Through following multiple stages of your funnel, they eventually purchase. When they purchase, they are then put into a new sales funnel as you continue to nurture an ongoing relationship with them.

It's a great time to leverage the sales funnel methodology. Internet marketing has offered a way to put a sales funnel on autopilot. Tools and resources you leverage can help you create an automatic and systematic sales funnel that continually helps you find new buyers and convert them into clients. Then, they are inserted into a new sales funnel that converts them into a repeat buyer.

And all the while, you're doing something you enjoy and you're providing value to others. It's a beautiful thing.

STEP ONE:
THE eBOOK

Okay, back to that first information product you're going to create. The initial eBook you sell is the first of many products you can make available. A low price is important. You can set this price based on your goals but it's smart to make it affordable. It's going to open the door to larger profit margins later on.

It's also important that the eBook provides value to the readers. Give them something worth more than what they paid. This way, they see and feel the value you've provided and they will be open to continuing a relationship with you and this way, you'll have a greater chance of selling products to them at a higher price point later. People will remember that initial sale you made to them and will use that as a benchmark for future dealings with you.

STEP TWO:
AUDIO PROGRAMS

Capitalising on your passion, you might decide that your next project will be an audio program. This is something that will either expand on the topic you initially wrote about in the eBook because you will be marketing to the same audience that was initially interested in it, or will provide an alternate option for people who want more than just the eBook (or an alternative to it).

Using the natural health topic as an example, perhaps your eBook was diet focused. Perhaps your audio program could be relevant to diet or wellness as well. You could, for instance, simply produce an audio recording of your book so that people can listen to it on their iPod or other listening device. Or, you could create a subscriber-based Internet radio program with health and wellness information. The possibilities are endless. As you research your niche, you'll undoubtedly find ideas.

STEP THREE:
HOME STUDY PROGRAMS

Some people want to learn something on an ongoing basis. Setting up a home study program could be the next step in your ascension model. Home-based studies are an ideal way to appeal to many people.

Setting up a course can easily be done via digital delivery such as email or via materials that you create and ship out to people. There are fulfilment houses that will handle the media production and mailing for you as well. You can gather this audience online and deliver to them offline. This helps you appeal to people who haven't yet totally embraced the digital

SELLING AND MARKETING INFORMATION ONLINE

mindset and who still want to receive something physical for their money. Home studies can involve text, interactive media, CDs, DVDs, manuals and printable copies of your eBook.

STEP FOUR:
MEMBERSHIP PROGRAMS

Membership programs provide the icing on the cake in terms of the ascension model and income earning potential. Why? Because the fee people pay is ongoing - provided you continually provide value and make them want to continue to be members of your program.

You could set up a private membership site where you continually share information related to your passion with people who want continued education on the topic. There are so many ways you could capitalise on the natural health niche, for example, that you could appeal to a wide audience this way. The monthly membership fee provides you with ongoing income as long as you want to continue to nurture the relationships in that membership site. Remember, you don't have to do all of this work yourself. You can assemble a team to help you.

The membership program sounds great, especially because it's the most profitable but unless you have an established presence, you're not going to be able to pull off selling this membership service. That's why the ascension model and the relationship-building part are so important.

As you've sold the great eBook that provided so much value for such a good price, and as you've continually communicated with your audience and provided them with helpful and valuable information, you've built a reputation that helps them see why joining your membership site would be valuable. Sure, some people might jump straight in at the membership but the vast majority of subscribers to paid membership sites joined because the mentor or guru was known to them and had already established trust over a period of time. By over-delivering on several products that were perceived as extremely valuable, trust was established with the client and a fruitful business transaction resulted from it.

Effectively nurturing a relationship erases doubt in the minds of the person reading the sales pitch about how valuable the membership site is. They already know that you provide useful and helpful information. Every product that they've bought from you was even better than the one previous to it and so they're stoked about the possibilities for this membership site and can't wait to see what value you are providing next. They just can't wait to sign up!

Wouldn't it be great to build a business where people think so highly of you? Wouldn't it be great to get to a point where you could mention something to your audience and they'd almost instantly agree with you and an overwhelming percentage would buy? It'd be fantastic if you earned off those sales. This kind of thing will only happen if you build relationships with people through providing effective and valuable products to them.

MATH EXAMPLES

So how many eBooks would you have to sell to earn $100K a year? Remember, the eBooks that you start off with need to be at an entry-level price point. You're going to start off with this lower price to attract people.

If you sold the eBook for $25, you'd need to sell 4,000 of them to make $100K. That might sound like a lot. But if you break that number down over a one-year period, that's about 77 per

SELLING AND MARKETING INFORMATION ONLINE

week. Once you begin to establish an online presence, that's not so difficult.

PRODUCT	eBOOK
Price per book	$25
77 per week @ $25	$1,925 per week income
52 weeks @ $1,925	$100,100 per year

If you sold an audio program, perhaps your pricing would be higher, say $49 each. For that level, you'd only have to sell about 40 per week to make it to the $100K level.

PRODUCT	MP3 AUDIO PROGRAM
Price per program	$49
40 per week @ $49	$1,960 per week income
52 weeks @ $1,960	$101,920 per year

If you were doing a home study program for $400, you'd only have to sell five per week.

PRODUCT	HOME STUDY PROGRAM
Price per program	$49
5 per week @ $400	$2,000 per week income
52 weeks @ $2,000	$104,000 per year

If you did a membership program at $29 a month, each subscriber would earn you $348 a year ($29 x 12). You'd only need 5.5 new customers per week to make around $100,000 per year with your membership program.

PRODUCT	MEMBERSHIP PROGRAM
Price per month	$29
12-month membership (12 x $29)	$348
287 customers @ $348	$99,876
Customers needed per week: 287 customers / 52 weeks	5.52

As you can see, the numbers to hit around $100K aren't all that outlandish, particularly if you're selling eBooks, audio programs, home studies, and membership programs all at the same time. It'll take a little while to get to where you've got an established audience who will be buying all of the above things but this business model is progressive, it's done on your own schedule, and with the help of others and the power of viral marketing, you could reach some significant milestones in a reasonably short amount of time.

By the way, did I mention that you don't have to do all of this on your own?

USING OUTSOURCING

You don't have to create all (or any) of the above products yourself. You could leverage an outsourcing model. Assembling a team of "go-to" people can provide you with great opportunities. Leveraging the expertise of others can help you grow your business without spending thousands of hours on it.

Freelancers or people who do work for hire can help you in many ways, including:

- Research
- eBook writing

SELLING AND MARKETING INFORMATION ONLINE

- Cover design
- Video production
- Website design
- Programming
- Marketing
- And pretty much everything you need to get your business up and running!

So, if you don't know how to create one of the information products you're planning to sell, that's okay. You can get some help. Paying someone a fixed fee to help you create something that could sell repeatedly over time will mean that you could realise a great return on your investment pretty quickly. Instead of spending hours and hours toiling over learning how to do something that you're not an expert in, you could spend a minimal amount of money getting that task done for your business. That one payment could generate amazing results.

Many successful entrepreneurs seem to be able to do it all. In reality many of them don't know how to do it all but what they do know is *how* to get things done. By using others' skills and consolidating a bunch of skills into a great product, you've got yourself something you can market and sell. And if it's something you're interested in and passionate about, you're going to enjoy the whole process!

OUTSOURCE SALES BY USING AFFILIATES AS SALESPEOPLE

Beyond finding ways to get people to help you create information products and then besides figuring out how to leverage the power of the Internet to sell your information products, you could also outsource some of the selling.

Affiliates could sell your products for you and this doesn't have to cost you anything. You could, in essence, attract a virtual sales force that will do promotions for your product for the promise of a commission if they do sell.

Remember clickbank.com? That's a place where you can sell your information product, yes, but it's also a place where you can get others to sell your product for you. The great thing about this model is that you only pay for results. You're not paying a base salary to anyone or giving them money when they're not benefiting your business. By sharing a portion of your profit with them, if they sell something, you could attract Internet marketers who already have an established reputation and a list of people to market to.

There are countless online entrepreneurs out there promoting other people's information products to their audience. Their mention of your product could result in sales for you. Why? Because they've established trust with *their* audience.

No sales equals no commission. And even if they don't sell, that's okay, too. Why? This isn't only going to bring you sales but it will also do a lot in the form of spreading awareness about your business and your information products.

Other Internet entrepreneurs will help you spread the word about who you are and their promotional efforts will help you in your ongoing efforts to establish yourself as an expert. Every person out there promoting your products for you helps increase your potential for profit without extra work required by you. Those affiliate marketers will send people to your website, your Facebook fan page, your sales page, your Twitter account etc. They'll extol the virtues of your product on their product reviews and they will talk you up to their audience.

SELLING AND MARKETING INFORMATION ONLINE

When you set up an affiliate program through a company such as Clickbank they will let you not only list your information product on their site but they will also manage the process for you. You set the commission rate (25 to 75%) and Clickbank takes care of the rest. Clickbank takes a small fee and for this fee, they collect the payments from customers, manage the payments to your affiliates, and they will digitally deliver the products for you as well.

Beyond listing your eBook on Clickbank, you could opt to sell it from your own website or another digital marketplace. You could even list it for sale on Amazon.com or the Apple iBook store.

As you can see, not only is there a real market for information products but there are a lot of tools and resources out there to help you with your business.

After you've done steps one through four (as mentioned above) you don't have to be done. You can do it again. You can create new products. You could find a niche that matches the niche you've chosen or pursue something new. It's up to you, you're in control.

CREATING PRODUCTS FOR LEAD GENERATION AND SALES

The world of digital products is expansive. There are many different digital products you can create, many ways to create them, and many ways to go about promoting them.

An eBook is simply a file that contains words organised in a way that is logical for the reader. There isn't a standard format you have to follow (although, of course, there are some best practices to follow). This leaves things wide open for newbies in terms of eBook creation.

An eBook can have graphics and pictures in it, if you want it to, but it's essentially just a document that's sorted into chapters. You can write it yourself or you could find someone to write it for you. What's most important is that it provides value for your readers.

You'll also want to write a sales letter that presents the eBook to potential readers.

The letter should follow some basic journalism principles such as:

PRINCIPLE	QUESTION
Who	Who will this book help?
What	What will it do for you?
Where	Where can you get it?
When	When is the best time to do it?
Why	Why should you buy it?

It's smart to read other information products sales pages to help you craft a strategy for appealing to your audience. Research into your target buyer and talking about the benefits of buying the product are important. Most of all, make sure the book is something you're proud to attach your name to so your customers will be happy with the finished product, will tell others that it's a good product, and will be more than happy to hear from you when you touch base with them again.

FINDING HELP WRITING THE eBOOK
Not everyone can write a well-crafted eBook. Not everyone wants to. There are a lot of writers out there who would be happy to write one for you. There are many classified sites, freelance

SELLING AND MARKETING INFORMATION ONLINE

forums, and online marketplaces where you can find people that will do work for hire agreements. You could get help in a number of areas related to product creation.

It's not always easy to find the right help. The cheapest worker isn't necessarily the best, nor is the most expensive worker. Here are some tips for interviewing and choosing the right help:

1) Check them out online. Look up that person's name to see what work you can find and to see whether or not you can find anything positive or negative about them. If it's a web designer, you should be able to find great examples of their work. If it's a ghost writer, you should also take a close look at samples of their work and their resumé. Perhaps it will be important to you to find a writer who is specialised on the topic you're passionate about.

2) Ask for an interview either on the phone or via Skype. This can help you determine whether or not the person is the right fit.

3) Be very clear in your directions. Drawing up a simple contract is smart. You can find sample work for hire agreements online that can be customised to your purposes. Be extremely specific on everything from delivery milestones, payment amounts, revision policies, and non-disclosure agreements.

4) Trust your instinct. When dealing with someone, pay close attention to their professionalism or lack thereof. If something doesn't seem right, listen to your gut.

5) Consider doing a very small project to gauge results. Instead of paying a ghost writer to write your whole book and waiting for it, ask for a sample article on your topic. Pay for it as well

(most professionals won't work for free). If you're happy with the small project, consider doing a larger one.

6) Set up milestones throughout the scope of the project. This will help you keep things moving in the right direction and will help you manage costs. If you get to the second chapter of having your eBook written, and it's not moving in the direction you had hoped, it's much easier to change the direction of things now than it is to wait until the writer has written the whole thing.

7) Consider using escrow services to manage payment. This is a good option for larger projects that you're doing with a new person, for example. The funds will be held in an account until both parties agree that the project is complete.

You can find people by placing ads online on classified sites, by searching for freelancer job boards (there are several that exist by niche and many offer escrow services that are free to you, the buyer), and you can also find professionals looking for projects by joining web forums related to creation of information products. Many of these forums exist and some have sections dedicated to listing "wanted" ads or to listing services available that are related to the information products creation field.

One place you can access outsourcing resources is Elance: http://www.elance.com.

HAVING THE eBOOK CREATED

Whether writing some or all of it on your own or having it created, here are some basics to follow:

- You can find a wealth of information online. You can also look offline in a local library to gather information for putting the book together.

SELLING AND MARKETING INFORMATION ONLINE

- Separate it into chapters and outline subsections to help you assemble the book. If you're working with someone and you are outsourcing some or all of the writing to them, the outline of the eBook will help ensure that it is a complete piece of work. You can do the outline or make an outline pitch part of their fee. They gather research and submit an outline to you for approval before they start the project.

- Be careful you (or your helper) don't plagiarise anyone in the book. Remember, it will have your name on the cover and you'll be responsible. Carefully cite sources and don't allow the actual copying of any sections. The same goes for images. You can purchase royalty-free images for the book or supply your own images. You can't simply source images from the Internet and use them as they may be subject to copyright laws.

- In terms of research, it's important to verify information with more than one source before taking it as gospel. Wikipedia.org, for instance, is a common research resource but it's edited by the general online community and just because something is written on Wikipedia doesn't guarantee that it is true.

- Check everything thoroughly before you consider it a finished product. You need quality standards in place. Remember, your name is going to be on this!

- Be careful about absolute language and be careful to put disclaimers into your eBook. You don't want to subject yourself to any lawsuits because someone took your word for something and didn't profit, broke something valuable, or something of the like.

AUDIO AND VIDEO PROGRAMS

Creation of audio programs and videos is easier than you think with technology tools that are available to you. You can buy tools to help you with this and it can be as simple as creating digital audio files with the push of a "record" button and sending them out much the same way you would send out an eBook.

MEMBERSHIP FORUMS

Setting up a membership site is obviously going to involve careful planning. Assembling information to share with others isn't a small feat.

This is where your outsourcing team can really come in handy. You're going to want to be part of the presence on the site as you are the face or voice that people have come to trust but all of the work in managing the site does not have to be yours alone. You can hire moderators and administrators to manage discussion forums. You can create (or have created) podcasts, webinars, articles, books, and videos a few months in advance of releasing your membership program and schedule everything in. Technology tools and the skills of others can also be capitalised on here. Be sure to plan and prepare at least a few months in advance but with the ability to quickly add in breaking news in your niche. You want to be sure your information is valuable enough for people to keep paying that subscription fee on a monthly basis.

DELIVERING INFORMATION PRODUCTS

An informational eBook can simply be delivered by email as a Microsoft Word document or a PDF file. But you don't want to have to manually send these files. First of all, you're not going to be at your computer 24/7 and sales could come at any time. Second of all, you're not going to want to make people wait. You want a reliable and automatic delivery method.

There are many ways to do this including:

- Clickbank or similar digital marketplace

SELLING AND MARKETING INFORMATION ONLINE

- Amazon
- iBook Store
- Setting up an auto responder on your website that triggers a file to be sent after a specific action (such as a purchase)
- Have people land on a special *Thank You* page immediately after the purchase where they access the download details for your eBook
- PayPal - This is a digital payment processor owned by the eBay company and it's a great tool for accepting payments and can also be used to automate digital delivery.

RECEIVING PAYMENTS

The two easiest ways to accept payments for your digital products directly is through PayPal or a merchant account. There are many merchant accounts available that you can sign up for. PayPal (owned by the eBay company) is generally accepted as a recommended payment method and it's easy to set up. Most people who shop online have a PayPal account and if they don't, it's easy to set up quickly.

PayPal offers the added benefit of helping you sell to people without credit cards, which is often an online barrier for some. People can securely link to their credit card or to their bank account. In order to receive payments, you can also securely add PayPal to your bank account and this will allow you to transfer funds out of your PayPal account as well as in. Funds are generally transferred from PayPal to your own bank account within a few business days, making it easy to access the money you've generated.

PayPal also offers an easy way to set up subscriptions so that your members are billed automatically on a monthly basis and you can set things up to turn access on or off automatically - tied to that subscription payment.

ATTRACTING CUSTOMERS
Once you've got a great information product, such as an eBook created, how will you go about marketing it to the world?

MARKETING VERSUS ADVERTISING
Marketing is more than putting up an advertisement. Marketing is more than a sales pitch. It's about developing a brand that's valuable and that's valued by others. By marketing, rather than just advertising, you're going to find and retain more clients and those clients can become almost like brand ambassadors for you on social media sites.

There are many ways to attract customers. The best way to do it is to, metaphorically speaking, shine a light and exude energy.

Shine a beacon on your helpful expert skills and this can be extremely effective because people will be naturally drawn to you. People are attracted to energy and your energy is your knowledge on your subject matter. There are many ways to attract customers online with light and energy that generates profitable results.

You can shine a light on your product and you can also illustrate your expertise in many ways. This isn't done through hard sales tactics, nor is it done through spamming others. It's done through building a reputation, authority, and relationship development. Because you're monetising your passion, this isn't going to be difficult. In fact, it will happen naturally and you'll enjoy the process.

ESTABLISH YOURSELF AS AN AUTHORITY ON YOUR TOPIC
The right online activities will naturally result in people finding

SELLING AND MARKETING INFORMATION ONLINE

you where they look for information about the topic you are a specialist on. Through being helpful and providing valuable information to others, you will start to amass a following of people who are interested in your topic.

GETTING FOUND ONLINE

If you do a Google search on your name, what do you see? If you have any sort of online presence you will find your name on page one of the Google search results pages. If you optimise your name for search engines, you could, to a degree, influence what turns up on that first page. This is important from the perspective of helping people see that you are trustworthy.

If someone finds their way to a page advertising your eBook and they want to know if you're a reputable individual, they could then do a Google search on your name or your company name. The results that turn up will have an impact on how they view you and whether or not they buy what you are selling.

You can do a number of reputation optimisation activities that can result in your search engine reputation displaying you as an expert on your topic.

If you do a Google search on me, Sean Rasmussen, you'll see that the vast majority of page one results relate to my online presence.

If people look to find out about the reputation of me, there are many places they can look further for more information. A good portion of those places link back to places where people can learn more about me, whether it is via social media sites, my websites, or other people's websites.

The thing is, you can't *just* sell information. You have to provide some of it for free to give people a preview of the sort of things they can expect from you.

The other thing is that people will look into your reputation. It's important to brand yourself so that they find you and it's also vital to conduct yourself online ethically because bad news will travel - and fast.

Ways to optimise your name or company name are numerous. Some of the things you can do include:

- create social media profiles on Twitter and Facebook;
- create a LinkedIn profile (http://www.linkedin.com). This is a great professional profile directory that typically ranks very well online and provides great opportunities to display your professionalism in your niche;
- author a blog related to your topic and update it often. See the blogging section that follows for more info;
- publish press releases about your eBook and other newsworthy items to help you rank on page one for your brand or name;
- write articles for article directories such as http://www.ezinearticles.com. Be sure to create a profile on the site with your photo;
- offer to write free guest posts for high-ranking websites in your niche in exchange for a link back to your website.

Periodically check to see what comes up on the first few pages of Google, Yahoo, and Bing so you can see how things are looking and so that you can address anything that comes up that you aren't happy with.

BLOGGING

Most people have heard of blogging. If you're looking to succeed in the information products business, you'll love blogging. It provides an excellent way to develop a readership and establish

SELLING AND MARKETING INFORMATION ONLINE

yourself as an authority. It can provide a direct place to sell your products and even host your membership group.

Remember that you're going to want to become intimately involved with Google. Google loves blogs.

Blogs provide an excellent way to get found by search engines and listed online. They also integrate well with social media sites. Each blog post published offers you more opportunities to connect with potential and existing customers.

Creating a blog is simple. You can register a domain name with a site such as GoDaddy.com and get website hosting with Hostgator.com. Their systems are simple for creating a basic blog. If you're uncomfortable with this, you can hire someone to set the blog up for you.

WordPress is a blogging platform that's highly recommended. It's free to use this open source platform and there are many free templates to use for blog personalisation. You could also pay for a customised or premium template (known as a premium WordPress theme).

Posting on a blog is as easy as writing an email. Of course, there are more advanced areas beyond simply posting but it's simple to learn to use the basic features that let you create eye-catching blogs with photos and embedded videos.

Blogs:

- help your site get found by search engines and this gets traffic to your site;
- can be a place to sell your information products or can be a gateway to send potential customers to the place where they can buy your products;

- can handle subscribers and getting subscribers equals the key part of starting relationship marketing;
- integrate well with social media sites;
- help you with every facet of promoting and marketing your business model;
- are cheap to start and to maintain; and
- are interactive and this is very good for shining a light on your business and your expertise.

Writing regular optimised blog posts will help you build your reputation and develop strong relationships so that you can insert visitors into a sales funnel and continually nurture relationships with them.

Blogs should be optimised for search engines for maximum efficacy but it's important that like every other facet of your information products business, quality comes first. Engaging, interesting, and valuable content for your readers is the top priority. If you need help with blogging, you can outsource blog post writing.

PAID ADVERTISING

Some Internet entrepreneurs opt to pay for advertisements that drive traffic to your website or blog. This traffic could buy products from you.

You could opt to place a bid on specific keyword phrases related to your eBook topic and pay a fee for each click that results. It might cost you, say, 25 cents for the click but that click could result in a $20 eBook sale. Conversely, that click might not result in any profit. For this reason, it's wise to approach paid advertising campaigns carefully, particularly when you first start out in building your business.

SELLING AND MARKETING INFORMATION ONLINE

SEARCH ENGINE OPTIMISATION (SEO)
Google is the king of search engines; content is his queen. Google uses the content posted on websites to determine how to list their search engine results pages. So if you search on "fad diets" or "natural remedies for X ailment" Google's algorithm decides which websites are most relevant to you for those terms. By optimising your website or blog for the right phrases, you can get listed for popular search terms. SEO is a great low-cost and high-yield way to get traffic to the page where you tell people why your eBook is so good. It's also a great method for building your overall online business approach.

If you write a book about "how to lose weight fast" you could rank for that phrase so that if someone types it into their search bar, your website turns up. The free information you provide on your site or blog could result in a new follower who subscribes to your blog or your newsletter and, through building a relationship with them, they could choose to buy your eBook.

If your passion was boating and you oversaw development of an eBook about how to build your own boat, your aim would be to rank for the phrase "How to build your own boat" or "Boat building plans" or something similar so that you could get found when someone went searching for this information. Your blog might include all sorts of boat lovers' information that would interest and excite that reader and compel them to either buy the book or at the very least subscribe to your blog so that this could open the door to future marketing opportunities.

THE IMPORTANCE OF KEYWORD RESEARCH
Because SEO can be so powerful for bringing you free traffic, you want to take keyword research seriously. *Keywords* are the words that people type into Google when they are searching for something.

Optimising for the right words and phrases could be the difference between a page one Google ranking and a page nine Google ranking. You want to find highly searched words that aren't very competitive. You also want to implement a number of strategies for shining a light on your expertise so that you are seen as an authority by search engines and by the people that they send to your site.

https://adwords.google.com/keywordtoolexternal is a free Google keyword research tool. By using this tool, you can determine which words and phrases are highly searched in terms of your topic. This can help you decide how to structure your website or blog. By doing keyword research, you can create a strong content strategy for your site.

Optimisation with blog content, for instance, would involve some of these attributes:

- a website domain name that contains a keyword
- a permalink structure that contains the titles of your blog posts
- titles that contain keywords
- headings within each post that contain keyword phrases
- images with file names that are keywords
- internal links that are anchored with keywords.

CAUTIONS

Search engines are getting smarter. They have thresholds for how many times they'll see a keyword on a page before they categorise that page as excessive keyword stuffing, which could result in being blacklisted.

Readers are even smarter than search engines. This is another

SELLING AND MARKETING INFORMATION ONLINE

reason why quality and value for the reader have to be at the top of your priority list. Think quality first and optimisation second.

You don't have to navigate SEO alone. This is another area you can outsource to an expert. There are many SEO consultants and companies who can help you get found for the topic you specialise in.

SOCIAL MEDIA

Facebook is the most visited website online and there are many ways to capitalise on the fact that the vast majority of Facebook members visit the site almost daily.

Sites such as Facebook, Twitter, Pinterest, Stumbleupon, Reddit, Delicious Mixx and many others can be great tools for helping you build that online tribe we already discussed. It can help you draw traffic from search engines. It can help you find people to connect with, help you establish your authority on your topic, and can be a great relationship-building and relationship-nurturing tool.

You can use it to announce new products, to answer questions, to interact with others, and more. If you take a look at some of these sites and look up some of your favourite brands, you can see how some major companies use social media to their advantage. You, too, can do this. You'll learn a lot by following some of the big companies out there and analysing their approach.

PROFILE AND POSTING TIPS

- When you create profiles, use an image of yourself. Your aim is to connect with others and people generally prefer to connect with people rather than logos.
- There are several different types of social media sites. Learn

the ins and outs of every site you join so you can capitalise on the potential of the specific site.

- Create an effective profile and use your website URL in the profile so people who connect with you can find their way back to your site.

- Follow others. Social media followers are more likely to follow you if you follow them back.

- Socialise. Don't simply use these sites to push out promotional messages. Be interesting, engaging and helpful. Yes, do a bit of promotion but don't go for the hard sell. Instead of posting "Buy my eBook now" consider posting a link to a helpful blog post that you've written on your topic. On that blog post there could be a link or a banner that begins to try to compel the reader to learn more about why they would benefit from reading your eBook.

CAUTIONS

- Be careful about what you say on these sites. It's impossible to take something back after it's been posted because it could spread like wildfire and could harm your reputation.

- It's wise to keep opinions about personal beliefs off the page unless your topic directly relates to that belief system.

- It's easier to lose a follower than it is to keep one, as well. If you're on Twitter and post 10 times in an hour, you might irritate people and they will unfollow you.

- Remember that people may consider looking at your previous 10 updates to determine whether or not they want to follow or befriend you on the site so do your best to keep the quality and value ratio high.

SELLING AND MARKETING INFORMATION ONLINE

HOBBY FORUMS

Remember we talked about creating private membership sites as a part of your ascension model? Free forums are also a great place to augment your online reputation. By participating in free forums that are highly popular and highly relevant to your subject matter, you could enhance your audience-building potential.

USING FORUMS TO YOUR ADVANTAGE

Forums can be filled with people that fit the profile of your target customer. Those people could be interested in your topic. By interacting with them you could start to build a relationship with them. You can also find other experts and gurus and benefit from seeing how they manage their business. Hobby-related forums can help you continually build your knowledge on your topic. They can provide you with resource material when you outsource work on your information products to others, and they can be a great place to network.

Many forums also offer profiles where you can link back to your site and list your interests. Many will also offer you the ability to add links to your signature. Those links could direct people back to your website or blog. Those links can also serve as great search engine optimisation assets.

Every link that points to your website is considered a popularity vote to search engines that pay attention to popularity in aiding them with their indexing. Every post you place on the forum gives you a link to your website. If you're an active participant, you could quickly rack up thousands of links.

When posting on forums, be sure to follow the rules and guidelines of the site. Use this as an opportunity to share your expertise and you could build a positive reputation that helps you gather new followers.

VIDEO MARKETING

YouTube is in the top five of the most popular sites on the web. It is the second most used search engine after Google. People devour videos on their computers, their smartphones, and will even watch YouTube videos on television via their Blu-ray players. They also take videos and share them with others via social media tools and their own websites.

Producing video content has great viral marketing power and helps you shine a bright light on your business. Producing video content can help you share information with your target audience and this is another way to develop relationships. People have different learning styles. You can appeal to more people by offering a variety of media types for conversing with them.

A video can be produced with just you and your webcam or you could get more creative. You could outsource video creation as well.

Take a look on YouTube at some of your favourite topics. You'll see a lot of videos around helping people get information. Many of those videos will direct people to a channel of videos or to a website where they can get more information.

GIVEAWAYS OR FREEBIES

A great way to begin a relationship with someone who is interested in your topic is to give them something valuable for free. Consider writing a short report or giving away access to a free short course that can be done via email newsletter. This does two things:

1) It gets the user to opt-in to receiving future communications from you. This opens the door to future marketing opportunities.

SELLING AND MARKETING INFORMATION ONLINE

2) It gives you an opportunity to demonstrate your expertise and value. If they get something valuable from you for free, this helps the person see the potential in paying for your eBook.

The freebie can be as simple as "10 secrets to success with _____"

Writing even a five or 10-page report can be a great catalyst for building a future relationship. People sign up for your freebie, extract value from it, and are then more open to the possibilities of paying for the next thing you offer them.

EMAIL MARKETING

Whether you use a freebie report or course or a subscription, email marketing can be highly effective for building a relationship. As you amass a list of subscribers, you can use that list for many things:

1) Sharing tips and information to continually nurture relationships.

2) Sharing news about your business and new product launches.

3) Directing people to new online properties and /or promotional efforts.

Email marketing is subject to anti-spam laws. For this reason, it's important to use an automated tool to manage your newsletter subscription list. There are many tools out there that let you automate delivery and automate opt-in and opt-out. You can also set up automatic courses through this type of system that help you put your sales funnel on autopilot.

Some of the email marketing tools that are out there will give you important statistics and information about your readers, such as email open rates. Open rate statistics can help you plan for email marketing by learning which sorts of subject lines are most likely to be read, and so on.

AWeber, MailChimp, and Constant Contact are three popular email marketing tools.

> **TIP:** Don't only use email for selling purposes. Share useful tips and information with your readers. Help them anticipate new emails from you and you'll increase the chances of the emails getting read.

CUSTOMER RELATIONSHIP MANAGEMENT ADVICE
One of the most important elements of your ascension model is customer experience. If customers have a good experience in doing business with you, this will elevate your status with them. Strive to listen to complaints, to right any wrongs, and to be as responsive as possible.

Some information products business owners outsource a customer service desk to help them manage customer service issues. This might not be necessary in the beginning but is an option to you as your business grows.

It's important to monitor your online reputation so that you can swiftly address any issues that come up before they damage your reputation. It's also wise to monitor your online reputation so that as positive feedback comes up, you can shine a light on it by thanking someone publicly for their positive testimonial. Your publicly thanking someone on Twitter, Facebook, your blog, or your email newsletter acknowledges the positive feedback and

SELLING AND MARKETING INFORMATION ONLINE

highlights that feedback so that others can see that you do, in fact, provide value to others.

EXPANDING YOUR HORIZONS
The world of information products is huge and presents many opportunities to you for expanding your horizons.

- Conventions and events can open up, offering you an opportunity to expand your horizons further and sell more products in the process.

- Joint venture opportunities may come up where you partner with someone in a complementary niche and recommend their product to your online tribe and they, in return, do the same for you. You could also share profits as a result of a joint course, eBook, membership site, or other information-related initiative.

As you follow your passion and you share and network with others, you will become a feature in the places where people look. People will gravitate to your site and recommend your products to others. Your demonstrated value as an expert on your topic will have the potential to earn you money from thin air. And you'll enjoy doing it.

HAVING AN "UNTIL" ATTITUDE
Having an "until" attitude means that you keep going until you reach your destination, even if it takes a while and there are a few stumbling blocks along the way.

Attitude makes a big difference in entrepreneurism. When you get to make money with your passion, this can have a pretty positive impact on the way you feel.

It's important that you try to avoid getting discouraged while you are building your business. If you agree with positive thinking, then you know that keeping your attitude positive helps you attract positive results.

Because some people require a longer sales cycle and because different people have different motivating factors, a multifaceted approach to your business is important.

Some people see you online and buy from you instantly. Some people will find you repeatedly in their travels because of the way you structure your business and will eventually buy from you. No two information products business models will have identical outcomes so there isn't an A-Z success formula that always hits pay dirt when you get to Z.

Sometimes you have to go through the cycle a few times. Some people make a good deal of money by the time they get to the letter Q. It varies. But your "until" attitude and your passion for what you are doing will help you keep going.

Because you're going to be spending time building a business that you're passionate about, it's not all about reaching the pinnacle of success. The rewards happen during the journey, too.

Have a safe, fun, and profitable journey!

Chapter 7
BEING PAID TO SPEAK

"It's time to leverage your skills and get you the life you have been waiting for."

JUDETH WILSON

PROFILE

JUDETH WILSON

Judeth Wilson - "Australia's Leading Trainer of Trainers" - is Managing Director and Lead Trainer of Upfront Communications Pty Ltd and the Founder of "The Trainers Ultimate Toolkit" and "The Trainers Ultimate Business in a Box".

Judeth has started and built four successful companies on three continents. She has been at the helm of Upfront Communications in Africa, Europe and now, Australia. This is impressive considering Judeth is just in her thirties!

A sought-after international keynote speaker and business trainer for the past 15 years, she has presented to, and empowered and up-skilled, tens of thousands of people in that time.

As a corporate trainer, when she talks the likes of Cambridge University, Sanofi Aventis, Minter Ellison, Grant Thornton and Women on Boards, to name but a few, listen!

Judeth is the founder of "The Trainers Ultimate Toolkit" which allows others to start their own training businesses and effectively build a client base that enables them to earn up to $35,000 a month, even more, working only 10 days a month!

She is the author of: *The Inside Secrets of Powerful Presenters Revealed – How to Get Enthusiastic Applause, Even a Standing Ovation, Every Time you Speak*; *Become a Millionaire Working Just Two Days a Week*; and *Training Works: Better People, Better Bottom Line*, which is co-authored by a number of the trainers that she has mentored to success.

This entrepreneur first established Upfront Communications at the tender age of 21 in Harare, Zimbabwe in 1997. In 2000, she moved her business to London where she worked with some of the leading companies in the UK. She is now based in Sydney where she lives on the Northern Beaches with her husband, Douglas, and their small daughter, Chantelle.

Judeth has a passionate belief in people and developing the skills they have. Her calling is teaching people the business of speaking and training, showing them how to easily monetise their skill and experience.

BEING PAID TO SPEAK

HOW TO EARN UP TO $350,000 A YEAR WORKING JUST 10 DAYS A MONTH!

Welcome to the seven steps to running your own lucrative business as a trainer!

STEP ONE:
DECIDE IF YOU WANT A SLICE OF THE "BEST CAREER IN THE WORLD!"

The freelance training business is a little-known, but amazingly lucrative business that pretty much anyone can be successful with. It's a business where there's huge demand from high-paying, quality clients and yet hardly anyone knows about it. You can make big money while working from home and choosing the hours you work.

Typically, I train 10 days a month and make over $35,000 each month doing that. I'm booked up months in advance.

For the past 15 years, I've been able to work as and when I choose for very good money because I'm a corporate trainer. I go into companies and work with small groups of staff and develop their people skills: anything from presentation skills, time management, exceptional customer service, selling and many other "people skills" programs. I up-skill businesses. This allows me to wake up each and every morning and do exactly what I love. I have to pinch myself whenever I think back to how lucky I have been to have fallen into this career so easily

JUDETH WILSON

and I am going to give you the information you need to be able to do it yourself too if this is something that excites you.

I have set up highly successful training businesses for myself on three different continents (Africa, Europe and Australia) so I am now in a position to show others exactly how to do the same thing for themselves. It has been so rewarding to equip people who are truly passionate about speaking, teaching or training and to watch them become successful in businesses of their own.

CASE STUDY

Steve made $800,000 as a trainer last year

Steve Carey, Melbourne, VIC

Steve Carey is an engineer by trade and was passionate about learning to become a trainer but he had never conducted training before.

He signed up for my program three years ago and was a very diligent student. He simply implemented all that he had been taught and in the first year, he made $230,000. In the second year, he grew his business to $770,000 and that increased to a very impressive $800,000 in the third year of operation.

He made that money himself, as a "one man band" not with a group of trainers working for him. He is a lovely guy but there's nothing extra special about him; he simply realised he could use his potential and presentation skills to become a trainer that can earn that sort of money. Steve is always quick to point out that anybody can do it if they simply follow the steps that he was taught.

BEING PAID TO SPEAK

WHY TRAINING IS SUCH A GREAT BUSINESS TO BE IN

There are 101 reasons why I love what I do but, in order to keep this chapter short, I will just give you 10!

1) I get to work when I want to in a month instead of holding down a 9am to 5pm, five-day-a-week job. I am my own boss and I pick what work I want to do and when I want to do it. I fit work around my life rather than the other way around. For most people, work-life balance just doesn't happen because there's not enough time to get everything done. They're battling and struggling, perhaps they are balancing families at the same time as working full-time and it is hard! I SO appreciate this flexibility now that I have had my daughter because I have the best of both worlds – I am the mum who is free to take her daughter to swimming and music classes but I am also the mum who doesn't need to worry about money because it is coming in steadily, and in abundance, on the days I do choose to work.

2) I find it particularly rewarding. At the end of the day, when I put my head on the pillow, I realise that I could have changed the way a person sees themselves and their organisation and the skills that they have. They are going to do things differently, perhaps find things easier, from tomorrow, in their lives. I can have made a difference. That's a fantastic feeling - it's so tangible: the improvement, the difference I can make in the way people do their jobs or see themselves or relate to others.

3) Okay now, let's not forget the money! Businesses are happy to pay $3,500-plus a day because you're working with 10-12 staff in a room. In some circles $3,500 is on the low side now. So 10 bookings a month is going to equal $35,000 a month. You simply have to work 10 days a month to make

$35,000. It is win/win for you and the organisation: they're happy to pay you for it, because you're improving the bottom line of their business by giving their people the skills to be more effective, and their staff are doing what they do in a better way because of your training. You're being paid well and the corporates are happy to pay it because of the value that they're receiving.

4) Your overheads are incredibly low. The great thing is that you are delivering the training in-company for your client so you've got very few overheads. There's no room hire because you are using their training room or their boardroom and you have no catering to worry about because the human resources manager or the training manager will have seen to lunches, teas and every conceivable logistic to make it an enjoyable day for the delegates.

5) You simply arrive, train and leave! Your training session could be a full day from 9am to 4.30pm or you could be running a half-day session or simply a few hours of training. Either way you're in, you do what you need to do and you leave – and you're home in time to sit and have a glass of wine in front of the early evening news.

6) The variety in each day. What makes me really excited about what I do is how much variety there can be. Every single day is different. The diversity is amazing. Some days all I have to do is have a meeting with a client. One meeting for the entire day, that's what I need to do. On others, I'm at home. Perhaps I'm working on a course, putting together some new material or maybe there's nothing that needs to be done and I just have a day free. Of course other days are when the fun happens. That's when you get "suited and booted" and go to the organisation to run the training course. I can tell you

BEING PAID TO SPEAK

when you arrive at the organisation you are treated as an absolute guru (and offered wonderful cappuccinos!). They have full respect for you because you are an "outside person" being brought in. So delegates sit up and take note of you. "This must be important. I must pay attention here, because they've brought an expert into the organisation." We, who love the limelight, love those little ego boosts!

7) The ability to form long lasting, meaningful relationships with your clients when they know you well and you know them thoroughly and can relate to their organisation and deliver meaningful learnings for their team. Building relationships with your clients makes the job so much easier. When you go in and do the first training for the organisation and when they see results, and they like what you've done for them, they ask you to come back again and again. It's great when you have a client in Sydney who wants you to run a course and they say, "We'd like exactly the same course run throughout our offices around Australia," and then you get to run courses in Canberra, Melbourne, Brisbane, Perth, Adelaide and travel to each city on your own schedule. So there are heaps of opportunities for travel too if travel is something you want to do. It's a wonderful when one of your key clients phones you in January and they say, "Right, let's put the entire training calendar for the year into the diary." And I open up my brand-new diary and off they go! They say, "Each quarter, we'd like three sessions of XYZ training and then can you also do…" The clients that I have developed good relationships with can be worth between $30,000 and $60,000 to me over the course of a full year. Now you can see you don't need many clients if they're going to be worth $60,000 to you. You only need a few clients to have a really lucrative year if you're serving these clients really, really well. Most trainers can have six to eight good clients and that's all

JUDETH WILSON

you need. So you do not need to find a different client for each and every day if you want to work 10 days a month. They keep booking you because they get to know you; they like your style, your reliability and your content.

8) I get to deal with a range of businesses from small companies to huge multi-nationals. Interacting with staff of differing levels is fascinating and challenging and highly rewarding. Some of my trainers run successful training businesses and they aren't corporate trainers or traditional business trainers. You can make money teaching others on any topic.

CASE STUDY

How I helped Toni turn "hobby teaching" into a lucrative training business

Toni Salter, Sydney, NSW

Training doesn't always have to be confined to the seminar room and corporate offices. In fact, one of my trainers concentrates her work in and around gardens. Toni Salter came to me already with her own business in the horticultural industry. Toni trades as The Veggie Lady and was already running some of her own workshops teaching home gardeners how to grow organic vegetables in their backyards.

Although Toni's classes were popular, she felt that she wasn't reaching her full potential as a trainer - and neither was her income! When I told her about the income that other corporate trainers were receiving, she realised that there was definitely room for improvement.

The problem that Toni faced was her audience. Her business was mostly limited to the general public and her type of workshops meant that people would only pay for a "hobby" course. What Toni needed was to think bigger and venture out into the realm of staff development with her skills. I suggested that she stick to her niche in organic gardening and develop something that was specific to her field.

It was important for Toni to continue doing her workshops with home gardeners because this is how she honed her skills as a trainer and where she had earned the good reputation that could be leveraged into other areas. A tried and true track record earns great testimonials and opens the door for new things. The first thing she did was to put her prices up. Yippee! She listened to me! She learnt that her time and effort were valuable and her fears were soon quashed as she saw numbers actually increase for her class enrolments (I hate to say "I told you so" Toni ☺).

This flourishing trainer was also running a weekly gardening program for an organisation that has day facilities for adults with disabilities. When she introduced joint venture arrangements into the mix the doors really started to open for her.

Toni contacted the Australian Institute of Horticulture. She was already a member and saw that they were introducing a new Registered Horticulturist Program for continued professional development in the horticultural industry. This contact has proven invaluable for Toni's influence within the industry. She has since been recognised as Australia's first Registered Horticulturist, become a National Council member and is now involved with programming and delivering their industry staff development all over the country.

Toni took the approach of offering to write useful and relevant articles and blogs for magazines, websites and newsletters instead of paying for costly advertising. This helped enormously in getting her presence known. She rebranded her course with a more positive spin, taking away the idea of "therapy" and calling her program "Cultivating Wellness". She has now teamed up with other professionals to give expertise and validity to the program, including an occupational therapist, landscape architect, psychologist and qualified chef. The team now presents a package of training in wellness.

She set up a Facebook page called The Veggie Club appealing to gardeners and rapidly built up a membership list of interested people. She also listed herself professionally on LinkedIn. LinkedIn gave her new contacts from all over the world and keeps her abreast of trends in research and development that she can add to her training package making it more relevant and topical.

Corporate managers then approached Toni to deliver some holistic workforce training to enhance their employee engagement strategies and to offer stress management techniques through gardening. Toni has now advanced into corporate training in a whole new way.

Training doesn't necessarily have to be limited to face to face workshops either. Her training packages were reworked to be available online, so Toni no longer even has to be there to deliver them and simply offers email support for those enrolling in her programs, freeing her up to do the thing she loves most - tending to her own garden!

When Toni started out, by herself, running training for general public classes, she cancelled nearly every second class due to lack of numbers. Now she is sought after by community and corporate organisations alike and is booked for months in advance. Toni's charge out rate has more than tripled since she started training, and now she is able to schedule courses around her lifestyle and family commitments while enjoying the benefits of a higher, reliable income. Toni is looking forward to presenting her Cultivating Wellness program at the Australian Diversional Therapy conference and in the US for the American Horticultural Therapy Association conference later in the year. I am very proud of all she has been able to achieve with monetising the business while still staying true to her passion.

BEING PAID TO SPEAK

Back to 10 reasons why I love the training business...

9) The ability to travel. I have seen so much of the world (not to mention the millions of frequent flyer points I have accrued!) and I am paid to do it. Not only to the main cities but in beautiful vineyards and scenic mountain valleys. You don't have to travel if you don't want to but it is certainly an option if you would like to.

10) It is necessary to research the training courses really thoroughly and put time and effort into constructing them but once it is done you have good courses that you are then able to tailor and adapt for other companies too. As the courses evolve they get better and richer and you are able to make changes to make them appropriate for the group you are training in every session.

    You are also able to run half-day courses or deliver keynote addresses using just sections of the information you have for your courses. Once you have the material it is very easy to be flexible to suit the client's requirements. I have trainers that now run anything from one-hour sessions to three-day sessions with no trouble at all.

The opportunities are enormous and demand will continue to grow, even if there's an economic downturn (perhaps especially in an economic downturn).

Here's why…

- The trend for corporations to outsource certain services is well established and likely to continue. Many of my clients use me even though they have internal training departments. Now I am finding that some of the internal training units are being closed down as it is just too expensive to keep them going and companies are choosing to outsource their training requirements. This means they are using specialist trainers for the training as and when they need it. This is a far more cost-effective way of doing it. This is great news to trainers that run their businesses as freelancers.

- In an economic downturn, the pressure to make cost savings and keep a lid on staff numbers increases the appeal of outsourcing.

- At the same time, because of competitive pressures, companies need to make sure their staff are properly trained and as efficient and effective as they can possibly be.

It's no wonder that companies see the benefits of hiring outside trainers and will continue to do so.

In a nutshell, the business of training has these BIG ADVANTAGES:

- Extremely low investment to get started.

- Overheads are minimal. You can work from home and all the training is conducted at the client's offices or an external venue.

- Income potential is huge. As you've seen it's easy to make $35,000 a month ($350,000+ a year) training just 10 days in the month.

- Flexibility with your schedule, so you don't have to train in the school holidays or vacation time, and you have plenty of time for everything else you want to do. After all, life is for living and enjoying not sweating and slaving!

DO YOU HAVE WHAT IT TAKES TO BECOME A TRAINER?

- Do you have a personality?
- Are you a "people person"?
- Do you genuinely enjoy helping others?
- Do you love the idea of working when, and how, you want to?
- Does it excite you to think about sharing valuable information with others?

If you answered "yes" to the questions above then you would probably make a good trainer. You don't need a string of special degrees or 40 years of experience to become a trainer. You simply need to be passionate about the idea of sharing information with others and have a willingness to run your own business and be your own boss!

> **KEY TIP:** If you were born to share information and help others, do it! Feel the fear and do it anyway. Some people think "What if it doesn't work?" but those who succeed think "What if it does?"

JUDETH WILSON

STEP TWO:
PICTURE WHAT YOUR TRAINING BUSINESS WILL LOOK LIKE

> ### *CASE STUDY*
>
> **Stay-at-home mum now makes more training for two days than she used to working a whole month**
>
>
>
> *Rachel Barnes, Sydney, NSW*
>
> Rachel Barnes was an IT trainer and new mum when I first met her. Over the past 10 years, she had to work full-time to be able to afford the things that she needed.
>
> When she heard about my business for trainers, she realised that there is a way that she didn't have to work as hard to earn much more money. She has now made a seamless transition into soft skills training. She's got the freedom to choose when to work, and how many days she wants to work; in fact, now she only has to train two days a month to earn what she used to be earning working for a full month.
>
> She loves what she does, and loves that she makes a great earning but still spends most of the time on what's really important to her.

There is a huge need for training in all organisations. Every single business out there, whether it's hospitality, car manufacturing, caring organisations, the financial sector or call centres (where there is a huge opportunity for training because turnover is often so high). This is excellent, because I go in, up-skill the staff, and in a few months all of those staff have left and you need to re-skill the new staff that have come in.

All of us tend to have had a job at some stage in our lives and from that job, or perhaps even many different jobs or careers,

BEING PAID TO SPEAK

you will have experience. Now with that experience, it's a great opportunity to become a trainer in that niche market. So if you've been in real estate for many years, you could become the real estate training guru. The money's in the niches, specialising in a particular field or industry.

There are more than 1.6 million businesses in Australia and all of them have people and those people need training. Every single business out there from tiny little hairdressing salons all the way through to blue-chip organisations have staff who constantly need to be up-skilled. So you can see just how much opportunity there is to do training in Australia alone.

WHAT YOU WOULD LIKE YOUR TRAINING BUSINESS TO LOOK LIKE?

- Do you want to run courses for individuals to come to or would you prefer to work in-company with a group of 10 or 12 people from one organisation?
- How many days a month would you, ideally, like to train people?
- What would you be able to do with the rest of the time when you are not training?

One of the best things about training is that once you have the training course ready to run the work is done. You just need to go and deliver it. You can put in as much or as little effort as you like. If you want to earn $300,000 a year, you simply do more training days. If you only want to earn $100,000 a year, then you simply do less training days.

Businesses typically pay $3,500 upwards a day for a training course. If a large client books you for 10 to 20 days a year, that means income of $50-60,000 from just that one client. You don't need many clients like that to deliver you a fantastic income. And once you've got a group of six to eight good clients, then you are able to simply maintain the relationships and deliver outstanding training courses and you are "sitting pretty".

If you are going to run public courses then typically you would be able to charge around $397 per person per day providing you can show a good return for their investment. So if you were to run training for a group of 12 individuals you would make $4,764 in the one day.

> **KEY TIP:** Training is the ultimate lifestyle business. Get extremely clear on exactly how you want your work life and private life to be and then focus all your energies on making it happen.

STEP THREE:
CHOOSE THE RIGHT NICHE MARKET

There is a great saying about niches that the best ones are an inch wide and a mile deep. I couldn't agree more. If I had my time again, I would be specialist trainer rather than the generalist I am now. You see, I didn't start my business with a plan, the training just grew and I started offering more and more training courses. And now, so many years later, I'm able to train so many different topics. And that, despite what most people think, is not the way to go. It is far better to be a specialist trainer rather than a generalist.

A good example is how much we are prepared to pay for advice. What you're prepared to pay an unqualified friend for medical advice would be nothing, you wouldn't part with any money if

BEING PAID TO SPEAK

they advised you to take a 30-minute walk every day, whereas if you went to the doctor, you'd be prepared to pay $70, or the equivalent, for a normal consultation. And if the doctor said, "You need to take a 30-minute walk every day" you would probably think you should do so because your doctor said so. But if that doctor referred you to a specialist, the key thing would be that, in your mind, you know you need to see a specialist, so you're not going to have a limit on what you would pay if that specialist turns out to be $150, $300 or $500. You've got to see a specialist because you've been referred from your doctor so you are going to pay that amount to the most qualified person. When the specialist tells you that you need to take a 30-minute walk every day, you are simply going to make that happen because the specialist has all the authority. The same goes for a trainer. If you find a niche and really become a specialist guru in that particular niche, then people are going to be prepared to pay for it because you are the specialist but, importantly too, they are going to listen to what you have to say.

I constantly argue with my trainers who think the way to go is to be generalists as they think there will be so much more of a market for a wide range of topics but it's actually quite the opposite - you can't be everything to everyone. Trainers who are multi-skilled and multi-experienced in all sorts of different fields often say, "But I want to show people how many different topics I can train and how much I know", and I say, "That really doesn't work. It's far better to choose one and to be the absolute guru in that particular area. Trust me!"

There are two ways to niche. The first is to niche into a specific training area, for example, customer service, or business etiquette or something that you are passionate about and know about, and then you don't train any other areas of training beside that.

The second is to niche into a particular industry, for example, financial institutions or engineering firms. Of course, this works better if you have particular experience, for example in banking, because then your marketing will show how you can "talk their language" having had experience in that particular field i.e. banking or working in financial institutions.

Top of the pops is "the niche within the niche" when you are offering only one particular training topic to one particular industry. And as long as it is an inch wide and a mile deep then you're definitely onto something. For example, if you're doing customer service for the pharmaceutical industry, as one of my trainers is, then that's a niche within a niche because customer service is just one of the many people skills topics that you could train. Only targeting the pharmaceutical industry means that it is narrow and so despite you thinking that it might be too narrow and worrying that there wouldn't be enough business in the market, as long as there are plenty of pharmaceutical companies that are willing to pay for your training, then you will be onto a winner. So an inch wide and a mile deep, that's when you're combining both a separate course and a specific industry to work in.

This is far better than people saying, "I'm sure I can turn my hand at customer service training and building teams and communication and all of the various topics under the sun." It is far more profitable to choose one area and to become the absolute expert and to know absolutely everything that you can and then position yourself as the expert that trains in that particular area and then clients are prepared to compensate you appropriately for up-skilling their team in a niche area.

CASE STUDY

Already a trainer but needed a niche

Kylie Warry, Sydney, NSW

Kylie Warry had been in health services and management for more than 10 years before she went out on her own. If you asked her she would say she "found" me and my program in October 2010 and at the time she was already in her own business working as a rehabilitation provider, completing training programs intermittently with a goal to build an established training business. Kylie had been dreaming about her own training business since 2004 but she had no idea of a niche market or of the value that she could bring to the market. She needed guidance and a blueprint to follow so that she didn't have to reinvent the wheel.

Kylie's background in rehabilitation focused on supporting individuals with psychological or stress claims in the workplace. Unfortunately she had seen the damage that poor communication can do to both individuals and to teams. The damage is usually completely unintentional but never the less destructive. Kylie had been working with the DISC model for more than 15 years so I helped her to niche fully into the area of miscommunication using DISC as a non-confrontational tool to teach individuals and teams about their communication style.

She now goes boldly where others dare to tread: she will happily find solutions for teams that are a complete mess. Kylie has gone from someone with a dream of having a training business to being able to charge upwards of $6,000 a day for training in the area of leadership and communication. You may look at that number and think it's high for a daily rate, however, the return on investment is a fraction of what ongoing miscommunication in the workplace can cost. Particularly if that miscommunication involves poor productivity, low team morale, potential bullying and harassment claims and high staff turnover. With this in mind the cost of training is minimal.

> **KEY TIP:** Think about a specific area that you could deliver training in. Now narrow the area down further. Now narrow it down even more. Now you will be starting to get close!

STEP FOUR:
CREATE A "SEXY" USP

It is important that you show a very clear Unique Selling Proposition (USP). It needs to be exactly that - unique. There are too many trainers out there who say they are communication skills trainers or presentation skills trainers or sales trainers. There is nothing unique about saying "we can help improve the communication in your business" or "we can increase your sales". You have got to show how you stand out from the crowd - that is absolutely essential. The USP is also known as the UBA in some circles. UBA stands for Unique Buying Advantage and it means exactly the same thing - how are your services unique and what is the buying advantage that people should buy your services over anyone else's?

We come back to the whole idea that if you are in a niche that's an inch wide and a mile deep, you are already going to be beautifully narrow; you are not trying to be everything to everyone. Contrary to popular belief you DO NOT want to be everything to everyone! You want to be a brand that counts for something in a very specific niche. Lots of trainers or teachers in a certain subject may say that they have the best course on "XYZ", but they have really got to show what makes them better, what makes them different, so that people making a decision on who to choose for training can very clearly see what makes you

BEING PAID TO SPEAK

different in the communication sector or sales niche or whatever courses you're going to offer. Just having a niche isn't enough unless you are the only one.

So if you're the oldest program in the market that could be a USP. If you're the newest, you're certainly not going to be the newest for very long, so that's not going to be a USP that lasts. If you are in a niche that is very specific then perhaps you may be the only one and let's hope that that lasts for a little while - that nobody else comes in to compete with you in that particular niche.

Too many trainers say they offer great service or they tailor the training. I hope you clearly understand now that those aren't USPs because just offering good service and just tailoring your program to the client is not enough, it's not unique. You've got to have an angle or an edge that makes it way more unique and, therefore, attractive.

A trainer of mine offers a "double your money back" on her sales training if your sales team don't improve by 30 per cent once they have followed each and every step of her proven sales system. She's adding a very tangible benefit (double your money back) - but only if they follow her proven system. She can do this because she knows that what she teaches works.

You also want to show your unique selling proposition in your tag line. A tag line explains what you do that makes you different. So a tag line would be written directly under your logo and your business name and describes exactly what type of training you do. So you have your business name that is specific and "says what it does on the can". For example, "Tick Tock Time Management Training" (I am kidding but you get the idea!). It's ideal if it has the word "training" in the title and then your tag line gives further description to your service. If you're able to show your USP within that tag line, then it's effective because people immediately can see your type of training and how you are different.

Too many people come to me and they show me a tag line that just says they do "empowering training services"; that's not clear enough because we don't know if it's personal training, fitness training, working with businesses or helping individuals to grow. You want to be very clear that it shows what you do but within that you want to show how it is unique and different from everybody else. Remember, you're not going to be standing beside your business card necessarily (to be able to explain it) when someone receives it because somebody could be referring you and giving your business card out to someone else. They want to read it when they get home or back to the office and understand perfectly what it is that you do so it needs to be particularly clear and obvious right in the first few seconds.

It is also not enough to just have branding that is unique or different. It is great if your branding does stand out but your logo or business card etc. alone will never get anyone to buy anything until you have built up immense credibility and brand recognition (such as the Nike logo or Apple computers). Of course, your branding must look nice and it's important that your tangibles reflect who you, and your business, are and how you are different.

You shouldn't spend months and months on getting the correct logo and getting the perfect branding design. I have a trainer who is still working on her logo eight months after she started. Crazy! Your brand itself won't make you money, it is the difference you make to the organisation, the training that is delivered behind the face of the branding – that is what makes you money and that's what people buy. It should reflect you and your style

BEING PAID TO SPEAK

of training and be appealing to your market so it needs to be relevant on many different levels and you want to be proud of the branding that you have because you're going to carry that through from your business card, into your webpage, into the stationery that you use and the workbook for your training course and the invoice and the certificate of attendance that you present at the end of the program. All of the above will be beautifully branded with colours and symbols that reflect your business.

Unfortunately, some trainers get too hung-up on it and spend months and months having it designed because they are not happy that it's not absolutely perfect. It's one of those things that "good enough" needs to be good enough as long as you can be proud of it, start using it and move towards setting your business up so that you can get paid as a trainer. It's important that you put your heart and soul into the creation of something you can be proud of and then move on and get monetising because it's going to be how you use the branding that actually gets your business rather than the branding itself.

> **KEY TIP:** As children we always wanted to "fit in" and be similar to everyone else. As business owners the key is to be bold and be different. It is the one time you certainly want to stand out from the crowd.

STEP FIVE:
FISH IN THE RIGHT POND

You need to market your services to an industry (or group of people or community or sector) that have both the money to pay for your training services and the inclination to do so. You should market where the business is. It's a bit like a person going fishing; you can't just stroll along the riverbank and stop and decide to put one tiny little fishing line into the river and hope you're going to find a fish. You have no idea whether that part of the stream is any good for fishing. You need to find out exactly where the fish are and then cast a net to collect those fish rather than put in a single line. This metaphor is exactly what we need to do to find business.

You can't just put an idea or marketing piece out there if you have no idea what sort of pond it is i.e. industry. Do they do training often? Do they have a culture for training? It's important to do your research first rather than just liking a particular industry or even having experience in that particular industry and hoping that the fish, so to speak, are going to bite.

There is a great story of a robber choosing whether to rob a convenience store or a house in a prestigious suburb. Of course he would be mad to rob the convenience store because there are going to be CCTV cameras in the store, the person behind the counter could have some sort of a weapon to fight back for self defence, and we know there's definitely going to be somebody there because a convenience store is staffed all of the time that it's open. Also, you're not terribly sure how much money a convenience store would have in the cash registers at any one time. Money could have just been collected by the guards and the attendants could just simply have small change left.

Whereas, if the robber chooses the mansion, when the lights are off and nobody's home, there's no CCTV camera installed in that particular house, and because the house is in a very wealthy suburb, chances are possessions in that house are going to be pretty good takings. I tell this story in jest of course and

I'm certainly not telling anyone to rob anyone at all! But the metaphor is a really good one.

The bottom line here shows you are going to work as hard to get training in an affluent market that can pay for it, as you will work to get training from an industry (or a sector or a community or a group of people) that don't have a culture for training. So it's important to think cleverly and do your research to find the right pond, and then it's a breeze to simply tap into that pond to get business.

For example, the trainer I mentioned earlier that chose to niche in customer service courses for the pharmaceutical industry is perfect because this industry is known to have the budget to spend on training and also the culture to want to develop its people. It tends to be very forward-thinking and knows that it's important to put money into people skills training. You want to look for industries that have a budget to spend on training; if they are too small (less than one million dollars in turnover), it's often the wrong pond.

I know a lot of people are very passionate about up-skilling and helping small business and that's a really lovely fulfilling business to be in because you can very often see the tangible result of giving back. But you often have to do public courses with a lot of individuals coming to a course from various small businesses and logistically you've got to do more because you've got to sell each one of those seats if individuals from different small business are coming together. On a practical level it's not as easy as selling just one in-company course.

If you find out that certain businesses have a good profit margin then chances are they would be able to train (and hopefully would want to train) their staff. But that's not enough; they also need to have a culture of training because they could have a huge financial turnover, lots of profit, a very successful business but no culture for training.

You want to ask questions and do your research such as how many days of training a year do they give individual staff? Some organisations do a day a year, others do 10 days a year (that's great because that's nearly one day a month dedicated to training). Some organisations don't schedule training at all in a year until a big problem arises and then they book training as a "miracle pill" whereas on the other side, some fabulous multi-nationals I've heard of allocate as much as 40 days of training per individual a year. That can include induction training and some ongoing, long leadership training and online programs but that's just absolutely tremendous that each person could have as many as 40 days a year of training that you'd be able to tap into.

Unfortunately some companies are tight with their money and simply don't develop their staff. You don't want to put your fishing rod into an industry, a group or a community that is tight and simply doesn't see the benefit of training their staff when there are so many other great, forward-thinking organisations and businesses that really do see a massive return on investment when they invest in their people.

KNOW CURRENT TRENDS
The trends in the training industry at the moment are for shorter courses run more often. In the past, people might have booked two full-day training programs, off-site and, sometimes, residential courses. Now, in most cases, organisations aren't pulling their staff off the job to attend two, three or five-day programs, because they see it as being far too much time away from the job. They are running shorter courses on an ongoing basis such as a two-hour session, which we could call a "learning bite", half-day sessions, from 9am to 12.30pm, or a full-day course which is usually from 9am to 5pm.

BEING PAID TO SPEAK

The good news with bookings that are continuous is that you're able to change the culture of an organisation if you go in once a month and make the learning stick and discuss with the delegates what they were able to put into practice from the last session, and you build onto that learning and skill base with every session. You may have a full-day program prepared and you may break it down into a signature course of blocks of two hours. So instead of a seven-hour day, you may have four modules of two hours each spread over four months.

The training that's hot at the moment is anything to help the team run a better, more profitable business such as sales training, negotiation and leadership skills. Whenever there is an economic crunch, people learn to run a "tighter ship" and they need to conduct business more efficiently and effectively using less resources - one of those resources all too often is their people. So the team that they do keep has got to be really super-productive in order to get the job done - very often the job of more than one or perhaps two people - so it is all about the bottom line of the business.

As trainers, more than ever, we need to show a clear return on investment (ROI) for the training courses we offer. Some courses have very clear ROI, for example, sales. If you are doing a session on "Closing the Sale", you can very easily say, "I'm able to teach your people the seven steps on how to close the sale and instead of closing one in 10 prospects , they will be able to close four in 10." That really is a confident return on investment that they are going to pay you $3,500-plus dollars for training because the return to their business could be a hundred times that. Another example would be negotiation skills. You're able to show that if you run a negotiation skills course they will be equipped to negotiate well and, more than likely, be able to save hundreds of thousands of dollars for your organisation as a result.

When showing a return on investment for the training course/s that you are going to be delivering it is very important to know the difference between "hard topics" and "soft topics". I don't mean hard topics in that they're challenging to deliver. We call a hard topic something that's tangible and easy for people to get their heads around and to see the return on investment. A soft topic is considered much less tangible and much more difficult to measure.

For example, a sales course or a session on closing the sale would be a hard topic because you can quantify the expected improvements; it is easy to sell the training course because you can outline exactly what the team will get out of it and the results they will achieve. On the other hand, soft topics such as customer service are often very difficult to measure. You can put a team through a day of customer service training but when they go back to the workplace, it's not as easy to measure the improvement. Yes their attitude and manner and their greetings and questioning skills will have improved if the delegate bought into the learning but it's very difficult to measure an attitude or behavioural change in a quantifiable way. You have to rely on performance indicators, for example, if you're doing a "Telephone Perfection" course and the telephone used to be answered within seven rings, and now it is tested and measured and the results show the telephone is consistently answered within three rings, then, of course, you can show that there has been an improvement.

Some subjects that are softer courses that just make the team feel better or have better morale are really difficult to measure and therefore, difficult to show a return on investment. I had a lady approach me a few months ago and she wanted me to teach her how to do art classes for corporate clients. I was curious about this and I asked her to explain further and she said she literally

BEING PAID TO SPEAK

just wanted people to go and have a space that they could express themselves and learn to draw and paint and just be creative for the day. I said, "That's a nice idea, however I simply do not think you are going to get corporate clients or businesses to pay you $3,500-plus per day to have people pulled off work to sit in a room drawing and colouring and expressing themselves - that's not how most serious businesses function." Unfortunately, she simply couldn't see that it was not viable. She said it was really important to her and I love that she is passionate about it and I can understand that she feels that it is important but businesses have really got to see a very clear outcome.

> **KEY TIP:** Do your research. Survey various markets and then train a topic that's easy for people to see the benefit they are getting for their business (or workplace or team or self).

STEP SIX:
CREATE CREDIBILITY QUICKLY

We all want success NOW and we certainly don't want to have to wait five or 10 years until our credibility is genuinely established because we've got enough notches in our belt and enough runs on the board having done training. However, I think there are clever ways of doing things so that you can establish credibility more quickly. Here are seven:

1) Have a presence on the Internet. This really is vital. People can be introduced to you and hear what you do but then in order for you to be a "legitimate business" they want to see that you really exist. And it's crazy but simply having a

website and some sort of presence on the Internet tends to make people believe that you are a business in good standing. So it doesn't have to be fancy, big, "best website ever created"; it literally does just need to be a presence that clearly shows your niche and your USP so people sense that you have been established for a while and didn't create this business yesterday.

2) Speak at anything and everything. When you are first starting out, it is so important to build your reputation in any way possible. You literally want to put your hand up and volunteer to do things for free initially just to get yourself known, to get your reputation out there and it's going to help to build your confidence massively. So think of all of the different places you could speak at. You could deliver a presentation at the local chamber of commerce meeting, where you have a captive audience, mostly business owners, who certainly may be able to hire you for your training. Speaking puts you in a very powerful position because people think that you are the expert, the guru up on stage, and so they therefore listen to what you have to say. And of course, they then go to the back of the room to speak to you at the end, and you're able to give them a business card (and even more importantly you get theirs!) and then you are able to follow up in the coming days. It goes without saying that it is SO important that you knock their socks off when you speak. You've got to be extremely prepared and have done your research about who is in the room and what value you can add to them. Start looking for opportunities – even the opening of an envelope is a good start!

3) Make your business seem larger without lying. Of course I don't want you to portray yourself or your business as anything that it's not. However, there are cunning little

BEING PAID TO SPEAK

techniques that you can use to make your business seem larger. For example, if you use plural words on your website such as "we", "us" and "our" rather than "I", "me" and "my", then immediately it makes the reader feel that it is a well-established, larger business and not a "one person band". This certainly can be the truth because as you get experience you are going to find other trainers with whom you can joint venture with as they specialise in a particular subject and you specialise in yours. You will then have the ability to send out more trainers than just yourself.

4) Write a newsletter. This is the ideal way to keep in contact with your prospects and your customers. It's a way of showing them "the love". A newsletter doesn't have to be long and laborious; in fact, it shouldn't be. It should be short and succinct and can be easily emailed and it literally only needs to be one page, or one screen (without scrolling down) as it comes up on a computer screen, and most importantly, it needs to give value. You want to know your clients and be very clear on your niche and how you can show them the value that you can add to them and their business. So give them useful tips and techniques on things that are going be of interest to them. You can always put fun things in like a monthly joke or quotations that are relevant and pertinent. It does need to be at least monthly and some people even send out short ones weekly to remain "front of mind" with clients and prospects. They may not need training right now but who knows in a few months when they've received three or four good newsletters from you and are impressed by you, you will be the first person that they think of when they have a need for training arise.

5) Write a book or an eBook. This is so much quicker and easier than you think and there is no other way that establishes

credibility as well because immediately you are an expert on the topic when you have a book. An eBook literally is free to write because you can write it as a Word document and then you PDF it and just put a nice title cover on the front. And voila! It doesn't have to be long; it can literally be 20 to 40 pages as long as the content is good, solid and valuable information. The important thing to realise is no one ever throws a book away but they very often throw a business card away. So once you've given people your book, not only are you considered an author and a very prestigious guru in their eyes, but also it will sit on their book shelf and be pulled off from time to time and glanced through and may be lent to other people so your book really is something that positions you extremely well. It definitely needs to be written in the area that your niche is in.

6) Put articles onto the Internet. Putting relevant articles from your niche area onto the Internet can go viral if your content is very useful. That is what you want - information spreading around the country, and perhaps even around the world, positioning you as the person who knows a great deal on the particular training niche that you have chosen. It's important that you always put your website details on the article so that, as more and more people pick up the article and send it to others who would be interested, they are always able to find you and come back to the source. This is one of the ways you can build your list of clients or, ideally, they might immediately want to do business with you as they have an immediate need for training or be fascinated about the training topic that you run. So it's important to have a presence and be out there speaking and writing about your particular niche as no one will find you if you hide under a bushel.

BEING PAID TO SPEAK

Of course, another way of doing this is using social media, where you put useful, educational comments on LinkedIn or Facebook and grow a large following of people who are interested in your particular niche areas and you stimulate discussion that gets you positioned with credibility in the marketplace.

7) Use social proof. This is whatever anybody else says about you, because not everyone's going to believe what you say about yourself. However, if somebody else has said it about you this is the biggest form of credibility there is. We believe other people. So when somebody else is able to say, "I just had a training session with XYZ organization, and the trainer was knowledgeable, funny and approachable" then we believe exactly what that person said. Notice I used descriptive words rather than just saying "he/she was fabulous" - you need to be far more specific than that. You want to get a testimonial that actually drills down into what particularly worked. So not just "it was great, I really loved it" but specifically what was it that they learned? What would they be able to implement immediately? What was their style and did they make it easy for you to learn?

Social proof is anybody else saying the value they got from your training session. You must always give as much detail as possible underneath the testimonial. So for example, don't just say "Cathy, said such and such" or "Cathy S said such and such". It's got to be a real name, so always get the person's permission – in writing - before you use a testimonial, and then you want to give as many details as you possibly can. For example, "Cathy Pier from Mona Vale, New South Wales..." - that gives you more evidence that Cathy really does exist. The best type of social proof is a video, because then we can see and believe and really know that that person is real with opinions that matter. If you get an opportunity, record video testimonials because you can always transcribe them into written testimonials to use in other places in your marketing. The second most powerful would be an audio testimonial which you can put up on your website or in a CD, followed by the written testimonial. Not everyone believes a written testimonial but you can get around this by including more details of the person who wrote it so people can look them up and ask them if it is, in fact, true.

These seven techniques will help you position yourself and get credibility far quicker and the marketplace will want to snap up your services because you'll come across as a legitimate trainer. It goes without saying that you must have done your research and "know your stuff". If you're going to position yourself as a guru, then you certainly have to know your content left, right and inside-out. It's very important that you take the time to do the research, to read up everything on your niche market and to get hands-on experience by doing a few free sessions first to get your confidence up really high and some good training under your belt before you start charging money without being able to back it up.

CASE STUDY

How boosted credibility helped Dawn pack in her job

Dawn Russell, Perth, WA

When one of my trainers, Dawn Russell, first heard me speak, she was going through some major changes in her life, changes that had caused her to stop and ask herself what she really wanted to do with her life and what she was truly passionate about.

Dawn was employed as the sales manager for a major international airline and while airline

BEING PAID TO SPEAK

employees enjoy many travel benefits, her pay was not even close to that of other management roles in different industries.

Having developed some instructional skills during a six-year tenure in the Australian Army Reserve, Dawn had a good basic background in training and always had a simmering belief that training was something she was destined to do, but had never found a way to move forward with the dream.

Hearing me speak that day was a chance event for Dawn. She had been due to fly out to the USA on the start of a three-month world trip the day before the event, but had serendipitously decided to delay her flight to attend the workshop at which I was speaking. Suddenly she recognised that she was being presented with a vehicle that put her back in touch with her dream. She's since shared with me that she spent the entire flight from Perth to San Francisco writing her application for the course I run.

Dawn attended my course at the end of her trip, flying directly in from Paris to be there. The course introduced her to all sorts of possibilities, not just around training, but around building a successful business at the same time. Highly motivated, Dawn developed a clear niche market within the franchise sector. She still had her day job at the airline while she set the wheels in motion for her new business, working after-hours and weekends to get a website built, put her systems in place and more importantly, to write a book to gain essential credibility.

Self-publishing the book, *This Little Piggy Went to Market*, and using it as a marketing vehicle, Dawn continues to be invited to speak at conferences on the subject of local area marketing for franchises. In addition, her corporate background in leadership, customer service, sales and marketing means that Dawn is a highly sought-after trainer for large corporate entities.

These days, Dawn delivers training across Australia and speaks at conference events, not just in Australia but overseas as well. She is a regular facilitator with the Australian Institute of Management and has a burgeoning business that delivers value for organisations seeking a top-down change in corporate culture. She now gets to work with some fabulous people and has not once looked back since her decision to leave the airline in early 2011.

> **KEY TIP:** Remember, everyone has to start somewhere. You know far more than you think you do and it is often just a case of packaging what you know cleverly and appealingly.

STEP SEVEN:
USE "PULL" MARKETING RATHER THAN "PUSH" MARKETING

In any business there are two important aspects: one is the quality of the actual service or product you deliver and the other is the ability to market yourself so that you get and keep clients. Over the years of running my businesses I have worked out what the key factors are in each of these two avenues in business. When I first went into business I had to learn the hard way. I didn't know how to get customers coming to me. I just got new business on a wing and a prayer and I had no actual system to ensure that I would get more customers each month. Now that I have been in business and have perfected the system I know exactly what works and what doesn't. I don't have to leave anything to chance anymore. I know that if I complete steps 1, 2 and 3 then the result is going to be X. This is a far more efficient way of doing business. There is no room for gambling and "pot-luck" in a successful business. It is all about using a system that works and then constantly improving it.

BEING PAID TO SPEAK

"Push" marketing can be likened to "doing a hard sale". No one likes to be hounded and bullied into doing anything whereas "pull" marketing is getting clients to come to you rather than you pushing your services into their face. The key with effective marketing is to find out exactly where your clients are:

- What associations do they belong to?
- What publications do they read?
- What habits do they have online?

It is important that you don't guess. You need to do surveys and find out what they are ACTUALLY doing. Then, just as we discussed, it is important to find out where the fish are in the river; once you know, you simply put your net into the water in that place. You position your marketing in those places where your prospects "hang out". You put your hand up to speak at events that they frequent. You make it easy for them to find you if they type your niche into a Google search. It is crucial that you make yourself visible to those who are looking for the services you provide.

Research shows that people are prepared to pay more for your services if they come to you rather than you going to them (pull marketing versus push marketing). You want to position yourself with credibility and confidence so that you are literally "pulling" affluent clients towards you. Those who want the service you provide because they understand the benefits – and can afford to pay for them.

I have never done a "cold call" in my life and I certainly don't intend to. That would be a soul destroying task I am sure. Cold calls could come across as too desperate – that you really need the business – whereas if you take a business-to-business approach of making your services known through credibility-building tools, such as a book or eBook, or speaking for free, then you are positioning yourself in a non-desperate, dignified way. I have seen it work time and time again!

More than ever, marketing now is about being visible and building a relationship with prospects by giving value. You can offer something of value to the prospects in your niche area (what they would find valuable such as a free report or CD on the latest trends in a particular area of the relevant niche) and this way you are able to build your list because they will be happy to give you their details if they know they are getting a useful eBook or information of some description. Then you would send a newsletter each month to everyone on your list with useful tips and offers so that they "feel the love" and when they do have a training need arise you will be front of mind.

In order to have a successful, lucrative business it is necessary to market using a number of different media and mediums. For example, different media could be LinkedIn as well as in an online and offline human resources magazine. The mediums could be speaking at relevant events as well as having a stand at an expo for your niche market. I tell my trainers to have at least eight different avenues of marketing at any one time. I call it the "octopus" and I get them to strategically work out exactly what they are doing in each "tentacle". It is then crucial to test and measure each area so that you can easily work out which marketing is giving you the best results.

Your marketing doesn't have to cost a fortune. There are even free things that you can do such as getting coverage in your local newspaper or volunteering to be a guest speaker at local business meetings. All it takes is a little creativity and the determination to succeed.

BEING PAID TO SPEAK

Here are just some of the results from my trainers who have used pull marketing to achieve the following:

- One trainer had her first $6,500 day (previously she was on $4,000 a day)
- A trainer left my Train the Trainer Intensive on the Sunday evening and had her first booking by the following Wednesday
- One trainer got the opportunity for a contract worth $47,500 within five weeks of attending my live training
- A trainer already has 40 days of training lined up for next year - this year!
- A number of trainers have international training booked in the next three months
- A few trainers only need do two to three days of training a month to support their lifestyle and they can be home for their young families for the other 27 days of the month
- All of my trainers have fun, love what they do and lead self-fulfilled lives by helping others.

> **KEY TIP:** Market your business using a minimum of eight different media and mediums at any one time. Never keep all your eggs in one basket by relying on only one or two ways to market yourself. Test and measure EVERY marketing campaign you ever run so that you know which are working the best for you.

IN CONCLUSION

There are a number of you reading this chapter who know you were born to train and this opportunity has your name written all over it. I help people in exactly your position with my "Trainers Ultimate Toolkit" which equips people to master the training, marketing, business aspect and courses necessary for training. If that idea excites you I SO look forward to meeting you. Please do come and hear me speak whenever you have the opportunity because I am able to cover so much more in my live presentations.

If you are sure that you want a slice of this exciting and lucrative business, if you have a clear picture of what you want your training business to look like, you niche yourself into a very specific area of training, have a USP, know which pond to fish in, create credibility quickly and use pull marketing effectively, you will be onto a real winner! Then the examples you have read of people like Steve Carey, Rachel Barnes and Toni Salter won't just be stories of "other people" but you can meet them and relate to them when your training business is succeeding in the same way. I know they will all be truly excited to join you in a glass of bubbly to help you celebrate! As will I!

To your great success!

THE NEXT STEP...

"To know and not to do, is to not know at all."
Bruce Lee

Let me first congratulate you on making it all the way through this book. I'm sure you'll agree it's been well worth your while. You now know more about generating wealth through new business models than almost everyone else on the planet!

But there is a big difference between what you know and what you do. It's only what you do that counts.

I invite you to recommit yourself to becoming one of our 1,000 new Prosperity Millionaires. The reward is worthy of your effort. If you haven't already, be sure to register for your free seat at my next Ultimate Business Opportunity Summit National Tour Event. Go to www.BusinessOpportunitySummit.com.au/BIZBOOK right this minute.

And remember, as ice hockey legend Wayne Gretzky says: "100% of the shots you don't take don't go in."

We'd love to hear your comments and triumphs from the book, and encourage you to get in touch via the website.

A closing word from Andrew Carnegie, once the world's wealthiest man: "No man can become rich without himself enriching others."

I trust this book has enriched your life as it has mine, and I look forward to meeting you in person soon.

Stuart Zadel

CLAIM YOUR FREE BONUS DVD NOW!

For a FREE copy of my detailed DVD, **"Secret Strategies You Need To Know To Make Your Fortune In Property And Keep It!"** register online at: **www.TGRProperty.com.au/FREEDVD** using **Promo Code: NEWPROP**

This valuable DVD captures three of Australia's top property experts live on stage revealing their closely guarded secrets.

After registering your details my free DVD will be rushed to you at no cost or obligation. This offer is valid for Australian delivery addresses only.

But you must act immediately. This FREE DVD offer is valid for a limited time only. Once the copies are gone, they're gone. So get in quick before you miss out. Register online at: **www.TGRProperty.com.au/FREEDVD** using **Promo Code: NEWPROP**

Alternatively, phone our office on **Freecall Number: 1800 899 058** during business hours OR cut out the coupon below and post to: Stuart's FREE DVD, P.O. Box 1232, SUTHERLAND NSW 1499.

☐ **Yes Stuart! Please rush me my FREE DVD** titled "Secret Strategies You Need To Know To Make Your Fortune In Property And Keep It!" [code: NEWPROP]

Please complete below in CAPITALS. Note: All fields required.

Name _____
Street Address _____
Suburb _____
State _____ Postcode _____
Email Address _____
Mobile Phone _____

Cut out your completed coupon and post to:
Stuart's FREE DVD P.O. Box 1232 SUTHERLAND NSW 1499.